...AN
...AS

...PHANS

Sterling Publishing Co., Inc.   New York
Distributed in the U.K. by Blandford Press

Credits:
Musical research: Danny Griffith
Musical scores: Robert Goodnow
Lyrics: Danny Griffith, Max Morath, Dorothy Mackin
Photograph on cover: Photographics, Colorado Springs

Library of Congress Cataloging in Publication Data
Main entry under title:

Famous Victorian melodramas.

Includes index.
Contents: Under two flags / Louise de la Ramée — The two orphans / Eugene Corman & Adolphe Philippe D'Ennery — Hazel Kirke / Steele MacKaye — Music for the plays.
1. American drama—19th century. 2. Melodrama.
I. Mackin, Dorothy. II. Ouida, 1839–1908. Under two flags. 1983. III. Cormon, Eugène, 1811–1903. Les deux orphelines. 1983. IV. MacKaye, Steele, 1842–1894. Hazel Kirke. 1983.
PS627.M44F3   1983   812'.0527'08   83-4813
ISBN 0-8069-7766-3

The material in this book originally appeared in *Melodrama Classics*, Copyright © 1982 by Sterling Publishing Co., Inc.

Published in 1983 by Sterling Publishing Co., Inc.
Two Park Avenue, New York. N.Y. 10016
Distributed in Australia by Oak Tree Press Co., Ltd.
P.O. Box K514 Haymarket, Sydney 2000, N.S.W.
Distributed in the United Kingdom by Blandford Press
Link House, West Street, Poole, Dorset BH15 1LL, England
Distributed in Canada by Oak Tree Press Ltd.
% Canadian Manda Group, P.O. Box 920, Station U
Toronto, Ontario, Canada M8Z 5P9
Manufactured in the United States of America
All rights reserved

Contents

Dorothy and Lillian Gish in D.W. Griffith's Orphans of the Storm, *the film version of* The Two Orphans. *This photo courtesy of Lillian Gish, from her own collection.*

Introduction

This book is intended to help fill the need for a serious approach to an important segment of theatre history—melodrama. It offers to modern theatre groups well-researched and organized melodrama classics of the 1850 to 1900 period tailored for present-day production. These play scripts are three of the most popular plays of the era. All of them enjoyed long runs and featured star performers of their day. They played in the famous playhouses of London and Paris as well as in U.S. cities from coast to coast.

My husband and I first became interested in melodrama after we had purchased the historic Imperial Hotel in the then ghost town of Cripple Creek, Colorado in 1946. The hotel had been closed for two years during World War II and was seriously in need of renovation and repair. In the process of restoring the property to its former elegance and rebuilding a business, we searched to find a form of entertainment that would have been popular during the heyday of the gold rush. We found articles and advertisements in turn-of-the-century newspapers published in Cripple Creek which gave us a good idea of the entertainments that had been offered at the local opera house. These were almost equally divided among opera, Shakespearean plays and melodramas. In addition, the travelling companies presenting these plays almost always featured variety entertainment as well, with singers, dancers, elocutionists and musicians on the bill.

It was our good fortune to discover a troupe of young performers doing a season of light summer entertainment in the mountains of Colorado. They were engaged to inaugurate the first season of melodrama in the remodelled basement theatre of the Imperial in 1948. Their presentation was a modern melodrama rewrite that met with instant approval and success. As we did more research, we discovered some fine plays that had not been dusted off for production for many years. We found them in diverse places, from public and university libraries to the private collections of actors who had been involved in the original productions many years before.

I proceeded to adapt them for presentation on the Imperial stage. *Hazel Kirke*, *The Two Orphans* and *Under Two Flags* have all been produced successfully for two seasons of 150 performances each. The versions printed here have been rewritten and revised for production with a cast of 10 to 15 rather than the 15 to 30 required by the original scripts. Cuts and changes have been made to enhance their appeal to audiences of widely divergent backgrounds and tastes. Archaic language has been revised to be comprehensible without disturbing the flavor of characterization and setting so important to melodrama.

The pictures included with the plays are principally those of Imperial productions. Others identify stars from earlier productions. They will offer costuming and scene design ideas and hopefully give the reader a feeling for the style of these plays.

In the process of researching, selecting, revising and producing the plays that have been presented at the Imperial for the past 35 summer seasons, we have come to appreciate and respect the artists, playwrights, designers, directors and producers who have nurtured melodrama down through the years. We hope you share this feeling with us.

Under Two Flags

A Melodrama in Three Acts
as adapted from a dramatization
of Louise de la Ramée's 1867 book

CAST OF CHARACTERS

LADY VENETIA, the "Silver Pheasant"

THE COUNTESS OF WARMINSTER, an impoverished noblewoman, her
    mother

RENÉE BARONI, a forger's tool

CIGARETTE, Vivandière, soldier of France

BERT CECIL, alias Corporal Victor, "Beauty of the Brigade"

LORD JACK ROCKINGHAM, his longtime friend

RAKE, manservant to Bert Cecil

THE MARQUIS DE CHATEAUROY, Chasseurs D'Afrique

BARONI, proprietor of the bric-a-brac shop, and a forger

ENTAMABOULL, Arab sergeant

BEAU BRUNO, Arab soldier

YUSSEF, Arab soldier

TIGER CLAW, Arab soldier

SI HASSAN, a Bedouin

PAULETTE, a dancing girl of the "Ace of Spades"

BOUAMANA, another dancing girl

SYNOPSIS OF SCENES

ACT ONE

Scene One: Baroni's bric-a-brac shop in London, late afternoon.
    "Let us drink to the benefit of those we love—and to
    the ruin of those we hate."

Scene Two: Card room in Warminster Manor, the next evening.
    "Very well, you have the money and the girl!"

ACT TWO

Scene One: Ace of Spades Wine Shop, Algeria.
    "Tomorrow night then, at the Villa Aiyussa, at ten."

Scene Two: Same, the following morning.
    "It isn't wise to fool with Cigarette!"

Scene Three: Same, that evening.
    "Ah, he shall have more company than he ever
    expected!"

ACT THREE

Scene One: The Villa Aiyussa, later.
    "Then man to man let it be!"

Scene Two: Ace of Spades Wine Shop, the next morning.
    "Cigarette, child of the Army, soldier of France."

The first Cigarette: Lotta Crabtree created the role in an adaptation of Under Two Flags *which was titled* Firefly, *at the Boston Theatre in 1868.*

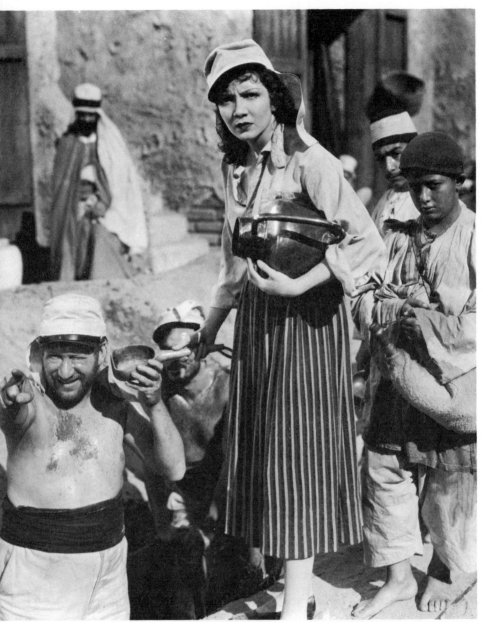

The last filmed, and perhaps the most famous Cigarette —Claudette Colbert —in Twentieth Century Fox's 1935 film.

About the Play

Under Two Flags was first published as a novel. It was written in 1865 by Louise de la Ramée, one of the most prolific writers of the latter half of the 19th century, who wrote under the name of Ouida. She also wrote the popular stories, *Bimbi* and *Dog of Flanders*.

Early records indicate that *Under Two Flags* was first presented as a play under that title at the Southminister Theatre in Edinburgh, Scotland on April 29, 1872. However, Constance Rourke recounts in *Troupers of the Gold Coast* that Lotta Crabtree played at the Boston Theatre in 1868 in an adaptation of the Ouida novel, *Firefly*, and that she was advertised by manager Junius Booth as "Little Fairy Lotta, the Diamond Edition of Dramatic Delights." Of her performance as Cigarette, it was written:

> The play was considered daring. Lotta was a *vivandière*, a mascot, madcap, rebel, who wore her skirts six or eight inches from the ground, and smoked freely and gracefully. She afterwards insisted that she learned to smoke from Lola Montez; certainly it must have been from that daring example or from (Adah) Menken that she received the impulse to smoke on the stage; yet she seems to have kept an air which it was not their fortune to maintain, that of innocence, which carried her past the increasing rigor of the sixties. In *Firefly* she used dozens of reckless small pieces of business with her incalculable air of distinction."

The term "vivandière," incidentally, was used in France to describe a woman who accompanied troops to sell them food, supplies and liquor. Probably Cigarette's mother, who was captured by the Bedouins, was such a one, and it was thus that Cigarette came to join the soldiers who raised her and made her one of them.

The first recorded New York performance, an adaptation by Paul Potter, was produced at the Garden Theatre by Charles Frohman and David Belasco on February 5, 1901. Here, actress Blanche Bates as the vivacious Cigarette was dubbed "a gold-tipped Cigarette" in a review by Alan Dale.

The play continued in popularity with such favorite stars as Maude Adams and Helen Ware as Cigarette. In 1912, Thanhouser Pictures made the play into a silent film. In a 1916 movie, Theda Bara played the sultry Cigarette. The last filming, by Fox Pictures in 1935, featured Claudette Colbert in the lead, with Ronald Colman, Rosalind Russell and Victor McLaughlin.

The evil Baroni gloats over the perfection of his step-daughter's enforced forgeries, as he plots to take away the rightful heritage of Bert Cecil. The Marquis de Chateauroy patiently bides his time, knowing that the fortune will then be his. John Storace plays Baroni, Nancy Duff is Renee, and Eldon Hallum is the Marquis in the Imperial's 1961 production.

ACT ONE

SCENE ONE

SCENE: *Baroni's bric-a-brac shop in London. The room is cluttered with furniture and antiques; shelves contain old books. The shop is dimly lit. Old volumes are stacked on a worktable U.R. A candle is burning at the table.* BARONI *is moving about arranging shop items, dusting.* RENEE BARONI *is at the table going through books stacked in front of her. She is a young girl of about 20, attractive, with a plain hairdress that makes her look older than her age. She is dressed in a drab skirt and blouse.* BARONI *is in his fifties, greying at the temples. He walks with a stoop.*

BARONI. Ah, you'll do well to mind what your old papa says, my girl. It's not wise to burn your bridges nor make enemies of anyone, for you never know from day to day who's up and who's down.

RENEE. And little it matters to you, so long as you can turn your profit!

BARONI. That's just my point, Renee, and you're a wise girl to see it my way. I have an appointment in a little while with young Bert Cecil, heir to the fortune and title of our great, good friend, the Duke of Chateauroy—

RENEE. And what do you hope to get out of him now? Isn't it enough that you blackmailed the old man into leaving you these books? You'll make a tidy sum once I've finished making them into autographed editions. Isn't that enough for you?

BARONI. Now, my daughter, surely you don't mind turning your considerable talents into a little security for your papa's old age.

RENEE *(explosively)*. As though I had a choice! Had I known in the beginning what you were forcing me to do—

BARONI. Enough of that, now. *(Holds paper over candle as though drying it.)* Ha, there's nothing like coffee grounds for making parchment look old. *(Pause.)* Do you remember the bracelet of Marie Antoinette that the young Marquis de Chateauroy was admiring last week?

RENEE. Well, I guess he won't be buying it now that his uncle has left everything to Bert Cecil. No one could believe he would completely ignore the French branch of the family.

BARONI. But he did—and so now it's Mr. Cecil who's got the money to buy the bracelet—and probably the Lady Venetia along with it, since he's the heir.

RENEE. But you told me she was engaged to Chateauroy—

BARONI. She was *(He hangs papers up to dry.)*, but now watch and see what way the wind blows.

(BERT CECIL and LORD ROCKINGHAM appear at door.)

The old Countess will never see her married to a pauper—

(Knock at door.)

There he is now. Run along now, Renee. Go for a walk in the fresh air; it will do you good. *(Pushing her toward the door.)* We have business to discuss.

(Exit RENEE. *Enter* BERT CECIL, *a good-looking young man, well dressed, with fine manners and speech, and* LORD ROCKINGHAM, *a British gentleman in his mid-twenties, well dressed in morning clothes.)*

BARONI. Ah, good day, gentlemen, good day.

BERT. I have come for the bracelet of Marie Antoinette.

BARONI. I beg your pardon, Mr. Cecil, but another gentleman is interested in the bracelet, and has made me a higher offer, which, you can understand—

BERT. Very well, how much is it now?

BARONI. Well, the other gentleman has offered me—

BERT. Never mind the act, Baroni. I have the money here. *(Pats pocket.)* What is the price?

BARONI. A thousand pounds.

BERT. Robber! Well—go and get it.

BARONI. Ah, we understand each other. At once, Mr. Cecil, at once. *(Bows and exits.)*

ROCK. That's a stiff price to pay for an engagement present, but if you ask me, it's only a beginning with Venetia.

BERT. It's no use, Jack. My mind's made up.

ROCK. Listen to me, Bert, you're a fool. Do you think she dropped Chateauroy and agreed to marry you because she's had some change of heart? No, it's because you've had a great change of fortune!

BERT. I tell you, you're wrong there. She accepted me before I ever told her about the will.

ROCK. Then you can be sure someone else told her before that.

BERT. Jack, I won't deny that her mother is grasping and ambitious, but Venetia's different.

(Enter RAKE, *manservant to* BERT CECIL. *He is tall and thin, about ten years older than the other men.)*

RAKE. Ah, there you are, Master Cecil. I've been looking all over for you. Have you changed your mind?

BERT. I wish you two would stop arguing with me. I've told you I'm not going to join up with you now. That's all changed. I'm getting married.

RAKE. What? Desert the two best friends a man ever had and jump the best regiment in the world for a woman? I won't let you do it.

ROCK. That's what I've been telling him, Rake, but he's blind with love and won't listen. As for me, since I've lost every cent I had, you can count on me to join up with you.

RAKE. Well, that's some comfort, at least.

BERT *(to* ROCK*).* You needn't enlist just because you've lost your money. What's mine is yours and you might as well share my good fortune as you have the bad.

ROCK. No, I can't stay here now.

BERT. Well, think it over. I'll wager you'll think better of enlisting.

ROCK. And you'll think better of marrying.

(Enter BARONI.*)*

BARONI. The bracelet, my lord. *(Hands him jewel case.)*

BERT *(looks inside, closes case, takes money from his pocket and hands it to* BARONI.*)* And here's your money.

ROCK *(to* RAKE*)*. Well, come along. There's no help for our friend, I'm afraid.

(They start to exit. Enter VENETIA, *"The Silver Pheasant," and her mother, the* COUNTESS OF WARMINSTER. VENETIA *is a pretty young woman, obviously upper class. She is impeccably dressed. The* COUNTESS *is an impoverished noblewoman. She has a most demanding air and expects to be catered to. She is elegantly dressed.)*

ROCK. Well, good day, Venetia. How do you do, Countess?

COUNTESS. Very well, thank you.

VENETIA. My mother wanted to do some shopping.

*(*RAKE *and* ROCKINGHAM *exit.* BERT *pockets the jewel case quickly.)*

COUNTESS. Ah, Mr. Cecil. How delightful to see you! I had no idea you were a collector.

BERT. Not a collector, really. I only came to look over some old books of my uncle's.

COUNTESS. Indeed! A bibliophile? Why, Venetia, I had no idea your intended had so many sides to his nature. Mr. Baroni, would you mind getting me a cup of tea?

BARONI. Tea?

COUNTESS *(very sharply)*. Tea!

BARONI. Tea. *(Exit.)*

VENETIA. I've often told you, mother—

COUNTESS. Yes, Venetia. But how fortunate to find you here. We've been wanting to reach you to invite you and your friends—Mr. Rockingham and—and—

BERT. And Rake?

COUNTESS. Oh, how stupid of me! I never can remember the names of servants except my own.

(Enter BARONI.*)*

Ah, here's my tea.

(Exit BARONI.*)*

BERT. Well, he isn't exactly a servant, you know—he's a friend.

COUNTESS. Of course. Well, I wanted to know if you and your friends could come to a small dinner party tomorrow evening.

VENETIA. Mother thought we could announce the engagement to a few friends.

BERT. How thoughtful of you, Countess. At what time?

COUNTESS. Let's say we'll dine about eight?

BERT. Fine.

COUNTESS. Then come, Venetia. *(Rising and going.)* We haven't time for shopping now, I'm afraid. I have an appointment with my attorney and—

VENETIA. Yes, mother, but if you will permit me, I would like to speak to Bert—

COUNTESS. Certainly, you two love birds must have many things to talk over and plan. I'll wait outside. Don't be long, dear— *(Exit.)*

VENETIA. I only wanted to tell you again how happy I am, Bert.

BERT. I pray that I may keep you so. Venetia, I have loved you for so long and yet I never dared to hope—

VENETIA. Everything is so different now—now that it's settled. It wasn't an easy thing, you know, after all my mother's hopes and plans with Chateauroy. She was so determined and we had such bitter words.

BERT. I know—I know, but I think she has come around now. At least, she's never been as cordial to me before.

VENETIA. You must forgive her, Bert, she has been nervous and worried about so many things—bills and creditors—not to mention the marriage of her only child.

BERT. I understand.

COUNTESS *(calling from outside).* Venetia—Venetia!

VENETIA. Yes, mother. *(Rises. To BERT.)* Come see us to our carriage.

BERT. I would be delighted.

(They exit. Enter BARONI. He goes to the table and spreads books out. RENEE enters from outside. She has a cape over her shoulders which she throws over chair, roses in her hands which she puts on table. BARONI goes to table and looks at flowers.)

BARONI. What's this? Roses—did you spend money for these?

RENEE. You know I have no money.

BARONI. Roses—in November! And your father toiling for a bare subsistence. *(Lights candle.)*

RENEE *(crosses and takes chair from side of table, placing it at back).* You'll gain nothing from telling me your troubles. Don't think you fool me, too. The money you make from forgeries alone will keep you comfortable the rest of your life!

BARONI *(threatening her).* You know nothing—do you hear? Nothing! I've taken good care that you know nothing.

RENEE. It's true the only schooling you've ever given me was enough to spell the manuscripts I write for you and food enough to keep me alive while I execute them.

BARONI. Renee, it grieves me that you should say such things about your father.

RENEE. Stop it! My father? You are not my father! You've made me a forger—you've made me a thief—but you are not my father!

BARONI. Ah, yes, what a comfort it must be to remember that your own father could never bless you with his name.

RENEE. He blessed her with his love, all the love she ever knew. Fear and misery were your gifts to her!

BARONI. How thrilled the Cecils would be to welcome you into the bosom of their family, the aristocratic Cecil family. *(Laughs.)* Especially your brother Bert—your half-brother Bert.

RENEE. Don't say that! Don't ever say that!

BARONI. Why not? What will you do? Answer me. What can you do?

RENEE. I can do nothing! You killed my mother with your slimy, threatening tongue, but I'm too valuable—too valuable to kill.

BARONI. So you are, my dear. Your mother—that's another thing. She never was any credit to me. Fourteen years barren until he took her! Miserable slut, we're well rid of her.

RENEE *(crossing to him)*. Promise me you will never let Bert Cecil know?

BARONI. And would I be so foolish? Haven't I been kind enough to keep him near you? Don't we enjoy his purchases and the profits on them together, my girl? Now, so that you can do your work, we'll just throw these roses out the window.

RENEE *(rushes to protect them)*. Don't touch them!

BARONI *(laughs)*. I know—you didn't buy them. They were given to you. Given to you by Bert Cecil, "Beauty of the Brigade," as some fool women call him.

RENEE. The roses were thrown to me from a carriage by the Lady Venetia.

BARONI. Whom the "Beauty of the Brigade" is going to marry. *(He goes to door, locks it.)*

RENEE. How do you know? *(Aside.)* Ah, what is it to me, a slave, a drudge! *(To BARONI.)* Vex me once more tonight and I'll not write another line.

BARONI. What is the matter?

RENEE *(sits at desk)*. My eyes. They pain me so. Perhaps I need a stronger light.

BARONI. There, there, my dear. *(Gets candle from window.)* The pride of her old father's heart.

(Knock at door.)

Who's there?

CHATEAUROY *(outside)*. Chateauroy!

BARONI *(aside)*. The Marquis de Chateauroy? What is the matter now? *(Goes to door and opens it.)* Come in.

(Enter THE MARQUIS DE CHATEAUROY, a young man of about 30, tall, slim, well dressed in morning clothes. He carries a hat and cane.)

CHAT. Ah, the same old shop, the same old curios. It reminds me of the cave of the forty thieves—and there is only one. Have you got something to drink?

BARONI. I have some cider.

CHAT. Cider. Ugh. *(Crosses to table near RENEE who is seated, writing.)* Renee, my pretty girl, do you venture out in the streets at night? Are you afraid?

RENEE. Aye.

CHAT. Here. *(Throws coin on table.)* Brandy, and the rest for you. Your father and I have business. We are in no hurry.

RENEE *(rising and taking coin)*. You want me away? Why not say so like a man? *(Looks at coin, shrugs.)* Why not?—like a woman. *(Takes cloak and exits.)*

CHAT. So, your daughter grows rebellious, eh?

BARONI. Women are queer cattle.

CHAT. So they are, but men are stranger. Baroni, in the variety of your occupations, there is nothing I admire more than your talent for manipulating ordinary playing cards.

BARONI *(makes deprecating gesture)*. So?

CHAT. And my cousin being of a liberal disposition, and always willing to cut the cards for a thousand or so, I have found the needle hole you make in the corner—to distinguish a low card from a high one—to my advantage.

BARONI. How many packs?

CHAT. Only one.

BARONI. One? *(Gets pack and gives it to him.)* And now?

CHAT. My cousin was here tonight.

BARONI. Yes.

CHAT. And bought the bracelet, the Marie Antoinette—

BARONI. Yes, for the Lady Venetia—

CHAT *(sits in chair at table, he picks up candle and holds it up close to his face, looking into flame as though reading fortune)*. Baroni—there is money in this candle.

BARONI *(rising and coming near, his eye on the candle)*. Money?

CHAT. Unlike most cavalry officers *(He moves the candle to the left.* BARONI *follows.)* I have not soaked my brains in absinthe. Having a head to plan, and your daughter's hand to execute, I think I see wealth for you.

BARONI. How much?

CHAT. I haven't settled on the figure. *(He moves the candle to the right.)*

BARONI. I would be interested in what figure you might settle on—let us say—

CHAT. Let us say about seven thousand pounds. *(He puts candle down on table.)*

BARONI. Seven thousand pounds?

CHAT. Yes, I think I will settle at that figure. *(Rises and follows* BARONI *who retreats toward chair at back of table.)* Sit down. Now, you knew how my uncle, the late Duke, took a fancy to my cousin Bert.

BARONI. Yes, they say he was in love with the young man's mother. He was at all times odd.

CHAT. But in spite of hearsay, he believed in me.

BARONI. He was decidedly odd.

CHAT. There were some who said that my uncle's moral sense was too strong to let him disinherit the French branch of the family, and that a later will would be found, in which he would treat me justly.

BARONI. Your riddle is still unsolved.

CHAT. He was a bookish fellow—took a fancy to those literary autographs of which your daughter's skill—pray accept my compliments *(He touches* BARONI's *shoulder with his cane.)*—has no difficulty in supplying. *(He tips* BARONI's *head with cane under chin.)* Now, when he died, he bequeathed to you a portion of his library. *(Hand on* BARONI's *shoulder.)* What then more natural than that, amongst the leaves of one of his rarest books, this later will has now been found.

BARONI. By you?

CHAT. Not I, but you, dear Baroni. You were the man to find it. *(Both laugh.* CHATEAUROY *rises to his full height, cane in hand.)*

BARONI. Oh, ho, ha, ha—no, no. There is only one improbability. You see, I didn't find it. *(Rises and confronts him.)*

CHAT. I foresaw the objection. *(Puts* BARONI *down again with his cane.)* And that is why I thought that the sum of seven thousand pounds, paid after delivery of the will, would make it clear that my uncle left his fortune to me and not to my cousin, Bert Cecil.

(Enter RENEE *with bottle of brandy, which she places on table and exits, returning at once with two glasses. She puts them on the table with the bottle, crosses to the table, sits, and begins to write, as if copying something.)*

BARONI. I am old and won't live very long. Renee must be provided for. But I—I am to run the risk. I must be well protected.

CHAT. Trust me. *(Takes out pocketbook, crosses to* RENEE, *takes out papers.)* Ah, Renee, my good girl. Here are a few papers. *(Places folded pieces of paper on table where she is writing.)* One of them a business form, this one a sample of handwriting.

RENEE *(looks at paper, then, to* BARONI*).* It's impossible—you can't! I won't! *(She rises.* CHATEAUROY *turns away.)*

BARONI *(pressing her).* Do it quickly or I promise our secret will be secret no longer.

CHAT. What's this?

BARONI *(soothingly).* It's nothing. Renee is tired; she has had a great deal of work to do.

RENEE *(writing).* Yes, a great deal. Forgive me.

CHAT. Now *(Watching her.)* see if you can—that's it, just like his own hand!

*(*BARONI *fills two glasses, hands one to* CHATEAUROY.*)*

BARONI. Let us drink to the trade of literary autographs.

CHAT. Let us drink to the benefit of those we love and to the ruin of those we hate. *(They drink.)* And to my honored cousin, "Beauty of the Brigade!"

BARONI *(looking over* RENEE's *shoulder as she writes).* Bravo, my girl, Bravo.

(He blows out candle. As candle goes out, the stage lights go down.)

CURTAIN

SCENE TWO

SCENE: *Card room in the winter palace of Warminster Manor, an elegant interior. Music, the March of the Foreign Legion, is heard softly at rise, becoming louder as scene progresses until bugle is heard.* RAKE *is seated at table playing solitaire, decanter of brandy and glasses on table. Enter* COUNTESS WARMINSTER. *All are in evening dress.*

COUNTESS. Why, for pity sake—Mr.—a—Mr.—

RAKE. They call me Rake, my lady. *(Rises.)*

COUNTESS. Well, whatever they call you—what are you doing sitting all alone playing cards at one of my parties?

RAKE. Oh, no offense meant, milady, and no discredit to your party, I assure you.

COUNTESS. Are you ill?

RAKE. Oh, no indeed—it's just that I'm not the sort—well, you see, I'm just more like myself when I'm *(Sound of bugle.)*—well—when I'm one of those.

COUNTESS. One of those—who are they?

RAKE. The Chasseurs D'Afrique, my lady. They start for Algiers tonight. *(On the words "D'Afrique," he stamps his foot.)*

COUNTESS *(looks at his feet, then at* RAKE*).* They do? Oh, the poor fellows.

RAKE. Well, they're not poor fellows. They're a regiment of the Foreign Legion, the finest fighting outfit on the globe. I for one wouldn't mind joining them.

COUNTESS. Joining that bunch of ruffians? Are you then tired of Mr. Cecil's service?

RAKE. Tired of Mr. Cecil's service! *(Again he stamps his foot for emphasis. The* COUNTESS *stares.)* Tired of taking orders from the man who saved my life in Asia? That I'm not, and Mr. Cecil could keep on giving me orders as long as it was his pleasure.

COUNTESS. Then why would you want to join the Legion?

RAKE. Well—it's different than the life I'm used to, but I can't go back to the old outfit, for I was courtmartialed for walloping a corporal who walloped my dog. Master Cecil, bless 'im, got me discharged and took me in his service, but after he's married, I'll feel like a blooming fish out of water.

(Enter BARONI. *He is not dressed for the party, but wears a shabby coat over the outfit he wore in the shop.)*

BARONI. I beg your pardon, Countess.

COUNTESS. Why, Mr. Baroni—I'm terribly sorry, but I simply can't talk with you now. You see, I'm having a small supper in honor of Venetia's engagement, and I must return to my guests—do forgive me.

BARONI. My apologies for the interruption, but I have urgent business with Mr. Cecil that could not wait.

COUNTESS. Aha! You needn't be sly with me, Mr. Baroni. I think I have some idea that looking over books yesterday wasn't the primary purpose of his visit to your shop.

BARONI. You misunderstand me—please. I must see him at once.

COUNTESS (*moves close to him and speaks confidentially*). Well, it's hardly proper to summon one of my guests . . . Couldn't you tell me, and I can convey your message to him later?

RAKE. Beg pardon, but if you wish, I can take a message to Mr. Cecil.

COUNTESS. Yes, of course, but no hurry, mind you, and don't disturb him if he's with Venetia.

RAKE. Excuse me, I'll see if I can find him. (*Starts to exit, stops.*) Ah, a perfectly lovely party, my lady. (*Bows and exits.*)

COUNTESS. What is it? Tell me at once!

BARONI. I really couldn't—well, you see, it's rather private, as it's bad news.

COUNTESS. Bad news? Well, good or bad, I've every right to know—after all, he's soon to become my son-in-law.

BARONI. Well, then, don't breathe it to a soul?

COUNTESS. Of course not—now tell me quickly—he'll be here—and I must know.

BARONI. A new will has been found, dated later than the other—

COUNTESS. And Bert Cecil?

BARONI. Is no longer the heir. The old man apparently had a falling out with him and a change of heart. The later will leaves everything to the Marquis de Chateauroy.

COUNTESS. Are you sure? How do you know?

BARONI. Only because I came across the will myself, put away in one of the old gentleman's rare volumes—

COUNTESS. And you have it? Are you certain there can be no doubt?

BARONI. None whatsoever. (*Takes out will and shows it to her.*) I have the document with me here—

COUNTESS (*backs up and pushes* BARONI *back.* BARONI *follows very closely*). Oh, excuse me—I'll see if I can find Mr. Cecil. Oh, how terrible—for him, I mean . . . I'll send him right away. (*Exits hurriedly.*)

(*Enter* BERT *and* RAKE.)

BERT. You wished to see me, Baroni?

BARONI. Yes, my business is urgent—(*Indicating* RAKE.) and private.

BERT. He may hear anything you have to say to me.

BARONI. Very well.

BERT. Now to the point.

BARONI. A very disastrous point it is, Mr. Cecil. You know what a strange man your uncle the late Duke was.

BERT. Granted. Didn't he leave all his property to me?

BARONI. Yes, in the will he made three years ago.

BERT. And as he made no other?

BARONI. I am sorry, Mr. Cecil, but as you know, life has its accidents.

BERT. Accidents?

BARONI. I have discovered that the Duke did make a later will.

BERT. What?

BARONI. My dear Mr. Cecil, this evening, in looking over one of the old books left to me by your uncle, I discovered this later will bequeathing all his property to—

BERT. Stop! Don't give it to me all at once. Let me have it in driblets. It is not left to me, you say? Then who is the heir?

BARONI. The Marquis de Chateauroy. *(Pulls out documents.)*

BERT. Give it to me.

(RAKE comes up to his side and looks over his shoulder.)

BARONI. Now, cast your eyes over this. I came as soon as I found it in the old book your uncle left me.

RAKE *(looking at document).* Fight it, sir. The estate is worth it.

BERT. Oh, damn the estate. It's given me nothing but trouble.

(Enter COUNTESS, comes to BERT.)

COUNTESS. Whatever is the matter?

BERT. A new will has been found and I am no longer the heir.

COUNTESS. Can this be true?

BARONI. Here's the proof. *(Points to document.)*

COUNTESS. If my sympathy—

BERT. Thank you, but I won't need it.

(Enter VENETIA. BERT goes to her.)

Ah, Venetia, I believe the next waltz is ours?

(VENETIA looks at COUNTESS as if for instruction.)

COUNTESS. The Lady Venetia was complaining of fatigue.

(Enter CHATEAUROY. He comes to VENETIA.)

CHAT. First strain of the waltz—may I?

COUNTESS. Oh, you do dance so well, I think my daughter's fatigue—

BERT. Is this your wish, Venetia?

VENETIA. I believe there is some mistake. The waltz after this one was ours, Bert. *(She takes CHATEAUROY's arm.)*

COUNTESS. Pardon a mother's enthusiasm, but I think they make the handsomest couple. Mr. Baroni, I believe we have finished our business.

BARONI. Yes, Countess. *(Exits.)*

COUNTESS. Mr. Rake.

RAKE. Yes, Countess. *(Exits.)*

COUNTESS. Mr. Cecil, as we are both people of the world, I may speak plainly to you. You have not the means to support a girl of Venetia's luxurious habits, and I am sure you are too much of a gentleman to hold her to an engagement that would bring only misery to you both.

BERT. Did Venetia wish to tell me this?

COUNTESS. Venetia's wishes have always been identical with—

BERT. Not another word! Is Venetia in accord with breaking faith with me?

COUNTESS. I understand your excitement and overlook the extravagance of your language, but Venetia desires me to tell you that she considers her engagement with you at an end. *(Exits.)*

(BERT *stands by table with head bowed. Enter* RAKE *with jewel case. He hands it to* BERT.)

RAKE. Mr. Cecil.

BERT *(taking case)*. There will be no need of this now.

(Exit RAKE.)

It was the token of our love. *(Sits in chair, head in hands.)*

(Enter ROCKINGHAM, *with a dish of salad, eating it. He sees* BERT.)

ROCK. What's the matter, Bert, not feeling well?

BERT. Never felt better in my life.

ROCK. Have some salad.

BERT. No, thank you, I'm not hungry. I'll try a drink of brandy. *(Pours and drinks.)*

ROCK. It will do you good.

BERT. I feel as careless and indifferent —

ROCK. What about?

BERT. And as for Chateauroy —

ROCK. What has he been up to now?

BERT. I'll do it. *(Pours and drinks again.)* In a week's time, we'll be back at the old stand, booted with light hose, and mounting guard.

ROCK. Not I. In a week's time, I will have vanished from the earth, known only as private so-and-so, Chasseurs D'Afrique.

BERT. Then you mean business?

ROCK. Indeed I do. I'm going to enlist tonight.

BERT. Count me in.

ROCK. What?

BERT. I am going with you.

ROCK. You mean she threw you?

BERT. No, not exactly.

ROCK. Her mamma then?

BERT. That's nearer—my fortune has gone up in smoke.

ROCK. How's that?

BERT. Another will has been found. Chateauroy gets the cash and Lady Warminster has informed me that my engagement with Venetia is at an end.

ROCK. And you would quit because of a mercenary old woman?

BERT. You were right, Jack. She's a chip off the old block.

ROCK. Well, I'm sorry, old chap, but I'm glad you found out in time. Either one of them would barter their immortal souls for cash.

BERT *(looking off)*. There's Venetia now, dancing with Chateauroy, all aglow with happiness, while I—*(Takes pocketbook from pocket.)* Well, this pocketbook contains every cent I have in the world.

(Enter CHATEAUROY. *He hears the last of* BERT's *speech, throws pocketbook on table.)*

CHAT. Are you in the mood for a friendly little game?

BERT. I don't understand you.

CHAT. We are cousins, after all our differences, you know. When I needed a thousand, you were always willing to cut the cards. If I won, you paid like the Bank of England. If I lost, you said nothing about it. Come—I'll cut the cards with you. How much is in the pocketbook?

BERT. Four hundred pounds.

CHAT. Let's cut four times, a hundred a cut—what do you say?

BERT. All right, get the cards.

CHAT. Here. *(Takes pack from pocket.)*

ROCK. Play carefully.

BERT. Never mind. I'm feeling lucky now.

ROCK. Well, take my advice. There's more in this than reaches the eye. *(*BERT *sits at table opposite* CHATEAUROY. *His pocketbook and the jewel case are on the table.)*

CHAT. Now, my dear cousin—remember I am lucky with cards—

BERT. At times—deal.

CHAT. I've occasioned some success with the ladies, too, you know. Lowest wins?

BERT. As you please.

*(*CHATEAUROY *cuts the cards;* BERT *cuts, too.* CHATEAUROY *turns up a low card;* BERT *shows higher card.)*

CHAT. Mine!

(They both cut a second time, same business.)

Mine again. What do you say, double or quits?

BERT. No, we agreed on four cuts.

CHAT. All right.

(Cuts again, same business. CHATEAUROY *wins again.)*

How much is left now?

BERT. One hundred pounds.

CHAT. Once more then.

BERT. All right.

(Same business.)

Well—you have it all now. *(Pushes pocketbook to him.)*

CHAT. I can't take it. I'll take your note instead.

*(*ROCKINGHAM *has been watching and as soon as cards are released, he sits and spreads cards out looking at them carefully, but pretending to play solitaire.* CHATEAUROY *does not take pocketbook.)*

BERT. I can't owe you money.

CHAT. Haven't I owed you?

BERT. That's different.

CHAT. Well, if there is any feeling—*(Goes to table and extends hand as if to take pocketbook, stops, turns.)* No, damn it, Cecil, I can't.

BERT. You won it, you must.

CHAT. Look, Cecil *(Pauses and touches jewel case.)*, Baroni tells me you bought a bracelet at his shop yesterday. Now give me the bracelet and we'll call it quits.

BERT *(goes to table and takes bracelet)*. You would lose by the deal. *(Hands him jewel case.)*

CHAT *(takes jewel case).* I know how to double its value.

(CHATEAUROY *picks up pocketbook and hands it back to* BERT, *who puts it in his pocket. At this,* ROCKINGHAM, *who has discovered the cards are marked, strikes table with his fist.)*

ROCK *(seeing that he has attracted their attention).* Solitaire—can't make it out.

(Very busy with cards, BERT *sits at table, lets head fall in hands.)*

CHAT. Aren't you feeling well?

BERT. Yes, I'm feeling well, all right.

CHAT. Our little game, I hope, is not responsible for your unpleasant feeling.

BERT. No, rather the reverse.

CHAT. Sentiment, then, perhaps. Well, if there is anything I hate it is sentimental memories.

(CHATEAUROY *tries to pick up the cards but* ROCKINGHAM *stops him. He then picks up the jewel case and exits.)*

ROCK. Bert—look here.

BERT. What is it, Jack?

ROCK. Press your first finger and thumb on the corner of that card.

BERT. Why, it has been pricked with a needle.

ROCK. What is it?

BERT. Three of clubs.

ROCK. And that one. *(Same business.)*

BERT. Smooth.

ROCK. What is it?

BERT. King of hearts.

ROCK. That one. *(Same business.)*

BERT. Ace of spades, pricked.

ROCK. So, there's the milk in the coconut. The lowest cards are marked.

BERT. But the pocketbook—why didn't he take it then?

ROCK. He wanted the bracelet.

BERT. The bracelet is of no use to him—of course! To give to—

ROCK. Precisely. *(Puts hand on his shoulder.)* This is a bitter bad job, a bitter bad job, Bert.

(Enter RAKE.*)*

Get ready and start for Algiers; that's all you're fit for now.

RAKE. Mr. Cecil, sir—

BERT. Rake—you know I'm beggared.

RAKE. What's the odds, sir, we're young, and there's lots of fun left in life yet.

BERT. Rich or poor, you've followed my fortunes. You'll follow them still?

RAKE. What trunk shall I pack, sir?

BERT *(rises and puts arm on* RAKE's *shoulder).* Rake—Jack—we start for Algiers tonight.

ROCK. Agreed!

(They shake hands.)

RAKE. We're off for Algiers.

ROCK. And I'm off to pack. We'll meet at the station at midnight.
(Exit ROCK *and* RAKE. *Enter* VENETIA.*)*

VENETIA. There's no mistake now—the next waltz is ours.

BERT. Your mother gave me a message from you.

VENETIA. From me?

BERT. Yes, and I asked her if you had authorized it. You bring me proof that you have.

VENETIA. How?

BERT. On your wrist. The bracelet of Marie Antoinette, that I bought in Baroni's shop. *(She puts hand to bracelet as if to take it off.)* Don't take if off—Chateauroy won it from me, no matter how. *(She still tries to take it off.)* Pray, don't take it off. Venetia, hear me for the last time. You told me that you loved me; it was false. You told me you cared nothing for wealth—that was false, too. You told me you could never accept my cousin—false, all of it, false!

VENETIA. Bert—wait—hear me.

(Enter COUNTESS *and* CHATEAUROY.*)*

BERT. Your mother told me that you wish to end our engagement. Very well, I accept the decision. I renounce you gladly. And remember, Venetia, whatever the future has in store for me, I will never hear your name without contempt.

CHAT. Sir—Lady Venetia is my affianced wife.

BERT. Very well, you have the money and the girl. The game is not done, and when we meet again, it will be where you won't have a chance to mark the pack. *(Strikes cards with hand.)*

COUNTESS. Leave this house!

BERT. Oh, I am going, but before I go, I will have the satisfaction of declaring that this latest token of your daughter's engagement *(Points to bracelet on Venetia's wrist.)* was won from me by a gambler's trick.

CHAT. Sir!

BERT. Aye *(Takes cards and crosses to* CHATEAUROY.*)*, and a sharper at cards! *(Throws pack of cards in his face and exits.)*

CURTAIN

ACT TWO

SCENE ONE

SCENE: *Ace of Spades Wine Shop, Algeria, a fancy Moorish scene. There are large double doors, the upper parts of which are glass. Arab soldiers are seated at tables, jugs in front of them, drinking.* PAULETTE *and* BOUAMANA, *in belly dancing costumes with finger cymbals and head veils, are dancing as the soldiers watch, drinking, celebrating. The Arab soldiers are dressed in uniform, bloused full trousers, faded blue Foreign Legion shirts, sashed at waist with bright fabric sashes. All wear turbans, except* YUSSEF, *who wears a red fez.* SI HASSAN *sits at a table with his head in his hands, apparently asleep.*

BEAU BRUNO. Wine! More wine! *(Pours and drinks. To* ENTAMABOULL.*)* And may the wine be better than the dancing.

YUSSEF. Wine improves all things.

BEAU. Where's Cigarette? Her dancing would be more to our fancy, eh?

ENTAMABOULL. Pah! Cigarette! You'd think she was a goddess! I say she can't dance any more than she can fight. She has you all bewitched!

YUSSEF. Not us, Entamaboull, but the enemy.

ENTA. Bah! You're all in love with her and have lost your senses!

BEAU. Where is she? Do you know?

YUSSEF. Gone to meet Billabee, the letter carrier.

ENTA. Well, I for one don't wait on her. This is a celebration. Now, three cheers for our victory at Zeralia!

(They cheer.)

And the brave men of the Chasseurs!

(They cheer.)

We will sing the Marseillaise, and if any African dog refuses to sing the chorus, I'll split his nose with my fist!

(They sing chorus of "La Marseillaise" in French.)

Well done, my brave fellows. There's not in all France a troupe more brave.

(All cheer.)

TIGER CLAW *(points to* SI HASSAN*).* There's one who didn't sing.

BEAU *(going to* SI HASSAN*).* He sleeps—wake up, there.

*(*SI HASSAN *rises.)*

ENTA. Here—this cup to your lips *(Puts wine cup to his lips.)* and sing!

TIGER *(putting another cup to his lips).* Aye, drink to our victory at Zeralia!

SI HASSAN *(puts up hands and pushes back cups).* No, for the love of Allah—I am a Moslem. My faith forbids.

ENTA. Sacre—what is your regiment? Turko or Zephyr?

SI HASSAN. Neither, sire, I am a Bedouin.

(General disorder.)

ALL *(drawing guns, revolvers).* Shoot him—kill him! *(Etc.)*

TIGER *(gets in front of* SI HASSAN*).* Wait, lads, the new Colonel arrived today. He is a regular martinet, and if he hears of our killing Bedouins for their religion, it will go hard with us.

ENTA. Then we will give him the lash!

ALL. Yes, the lash!

ENTA. Fifty blows will break every bone in his body—it will come near killing him anyway.

(Enter CIGARETTE *with mail pouch strapped over her shoulder. She is a beautiful dark-haired, dark-skinned girl, dressed in Foreign Legion uniform, knee-high boots, embroidered skirt over trousers, Turkish fez hat. Her manner is bold and her voice full of command.)*

CIG. And I'll come near killing you—my prince of bullies!

ALL. Cigarette!

CIG. Aye, Cigarette! I'll teach you to whip a defenseless man. *(Takes whip and lashes* ENTAMABOULL *about the legs. To* SI HASSAN*.)* Go in peace.

*(*SI HASSAN *rushes to her, kneels and kisses hem of her skirt. She makes exclamation of anger and points to door. He starts to go; the men stop him. She rushes and lashes them about the legs. They let him go and he exits quickly.)*

CIG. Ah, who hates Bedouins more than I! This man was one against all of you. I'll not have you spoiling the victory at Zeralia at the bidding of a drunken chasseur. *(She strikes* ENTAMABOULL *about ankles with whip.)* Now, there's more important business. Billabee, the letter carrier, is dead, and I have brought these through for you.

ALL. Dead?

CIG. Yes, dead. I rode up in time to hear the shots. They shot him and left him to die, but he kept your letters. When I came up, he could hardly speak with the blood in his throat. "There are the letters, Cigarette," he said, and he just turned over and died. *(She shrugs and opens mail pouch.)* Beau, here is one from your mother. She doesn't know what a bad one you are. Entamaboull, a love scrawl for you. That girl doesn't know you, eh? *(To* TIGER CLAW*.)* And tobacco. *(Smells package.)* That girl knows you. She knows your passions go up in smoke. And here's another—*(To* YUSSEF*.)* papers, commission—Billabee forgot nothing, and Billabee is dead.

ENTA *(puts arm around her).* Well, I'm not dead.

CIG *(pushes him away).* It's time you were—why is it all the good men get killed, while you—

ENTA. And if I were Corporal Victor—

CIG. You would know better.

ENTA. That dandy, with the soft white hands.

CIG. Which he keeps in his own pockets. *(She pushes him.)*

ENTA. He treats you like a china doll, and will throw you out the window when he gets enough of you.

CIG. Never mind—I can take care of myself. I can shoot a louis from between your fingers at twenty paces.

ENTA. Not mine.

CIG. Ha—I thought so, coward!

(Enter BERT in uniform of French Foreign Legion.)

BERT. Let me hold the louis. *(Comes to her.)*

ENTA. Yes, let the brave Corporal Victor hold it—he has so much faith in your marksmanship!

BERT. Oh, I have more than faith, I have the louis. *(Takes coin from pocket, tosses it in the air, catches it.)* Where shall I stand? Here?

CIG *(draws pistol and aims. She flinches, unable to fire, hesitates; soldiers watch).* I can't. I can't!

YUSSEF *(goes and takes louis from BERT).* Here, let me hold the louis. *(YUSSEF holds it out. CIGARETTE shoots. He drops the coin. BERT picks it up. All cheer.)*

ENTA. I've seen enough of this—come on, all fall in for parade.

(Bugle heard off. Soldiers line up and exit, talking noisily, calling to one another. All off except BERT and CIGARETTE.)

BERT. Jack and Rake have been out all day. They'll soon be here and hungry. Is there food for them?

CIG *(gets bread and cheese, brings it to table, picks up pipe and match).* Do the women in your country smoke?

BERT. Well—they draw the line at pipes.

CIG *(takes pipe out of her mouth, looks at it and puts it on table. She wipes her hands on dress.)* Do they swear?

BERT. Very mildly.

CIG. Do they shoot Bedouins?

BERT. There are no Bedouins to shoot.

CIG. Well, do they cut off enemies' rings on the battlefields?

BERT. Really—that's a peculiar question.

CIG. Do they wear their dresses short like this?

BERT. It is not the prevailing mode.

CIG. I see. Did you leave a woman back there?

BERT. Little girl, enough of this. While you are worrying over such illusions, I shall have some food. *(He cuts bread and cheese and begins to eat.)*

CIG. I know what she is like. She is like a silver pheasant, strutting around all day in the sun and admiring herself in the glass. She has ribbons, laces and flounces, and she combs her hair. *(Runs her fingers through her hair angrily.)* Well, I hate her—do you hear? And if I ever meet her, I'll kill her! *(Puts hand on revolver in belt.)*

BERT *(puts hand over hers and returns revolver to belt).* Now, now— you keep your killing for the Bedouins. You're a brave soldier, and you won the day for us at Zeralia, by bringing your soldiers to my rescue.

CIG *(has cross on breast attached to ribbon. She raises it to her lips and kisses it).* My soldiers gave me this cross for it. I wanted it so much. But more than that I wanted—I wanted—

BERT. Yes—and now, my comrades will want their dinner.
(She stamps her foot and turns away. Enter ROCKINGHAM *in Foreign Legion uniform with bag on back. He does not see* CIGA-RETTE.*)*

ROCK. Well, Cecil?

CIG *(aside)*. Cecil?

ROCK. I've brought some potatoes for us. *(Takes bag to* BERT.*)*

BERT. Fine, we'll put them in the kitchen. Come, Jack, we'll go and get some wine.

CIG. But we have wine here.

BERT. Yes, but in honor of Zeralia, we'll drink champagne tonight, and the louis you shot shall pay for it. *(Throws coin to* ROCKINGHAM, *who catches it.)* Come, Jack, we'll find champagne.

(They exit.)

CIG. Cecil—his name is Cecil. And there is a woman! Am I so ugly? I'll see—I'll see. *(Runs and gets glass hanging on wall and looks in it. She studies herself in different positions.)* Why no, I'm not—really, I'm not. Yes, I am, but there's no reason why I shouldn't fix myself up. I will. I will. *(Puts glass on table and gets bucket from back, also curry comb and brush.)* Now, we'll see what The Silver Pheasant does. I can comb my hair as well as she. *(Takes curry comb and knocks it on chair, as if knocking dust out of it. Then she brushes it with a brush. This is an imitation of a man using a curry comb and brush when currying a horse.)* I can comb my hair. *(Repeats brushing.)* There. And she keeps her clothes clean. *(Brushes jacket and dress.)* And she blacks her boots every morning. *(Puts up foot and brushes boots with same brush. She brushes hair down, rolls it up, goes and gets small fez hat, and puts it on.)* She has a little cap that comes way down over her eyes, I know the kind. *(She walks as if imitating a grand lady, looks at herself in glass, shakes her head and lets her hair fall down around her shoulders again.)* No, it's because she has ribbons and flounces and a long train, trailing on the ground *(Stoops down and walks so low, her own short skirt trails. She walks, swinging it behind her as a train.)* Oh, I hate her, I hate her. I can't have those things. *(Pause.)* I have to be feminine. *(Sits and puts foot across her leg and lights match.)* No, the first thing—*(Pauses, realizes what she is doing. She lays down pipe, uncrosses legs, sighs, folds hands and lets head drop wearily to one side.)* That's the first thing—I mustn't swear. Mustn't loot Bedouins—mustn't smoke. *(Takes pipe, looks at it, kisses it, gets up and throws pipe on floor.)* There—there—there—I'll only smoke cigarettes.

(Enter RAKE *in uniform.)*

RAKE. Well, little lady, what's all this?

CIG. Rake, oh Rake, he really doesn't care for me. There's another woman in his life.

RAKE. Well, if the Lady Venetia—

CIG. There, you've said it.

Cigarette (Georgia Loveless in the Imperial's 1971 production) contemplates how she might fix herself up and imitate her rival, "The Silver Pheasant." Most aggravating, she decides, is that she will have to give up her pipe and smoke only cigarettes!

RAKE. That's the name of a yacht.

CIG. I don't like the name, do you?

RAKE. I tell you, it's the name of his yacht he used to have in other days.

CIG. Stop lying—I hate her.

RAKE. See here, Cigarette, you're off on the wrong track.

CIG. I'm not—he loved her—he loves her still.

RAKE. Why don't you make him jealous?

CIG. I don't know how—wait, I do, if you will help. You fall on your knees at my feet.

RAKE. Don't be silly.

CIG. Come on—he might come in and see you—and—shoot you. *(She moves close, coaxing him.)*

RAKE. No, thank you, I don't want to be shot, even for you, young lady.

CIG. Please, just this once. *(She tickles his stomach. He laughs wildly.)*

RAKE. Well, I don't want to be shot even once. Besides, it would look so silly.

CIG. No, it won't, not if you do it.

RAKE. Look, I want to help you, but I don't believe in this kind of nonsense. *(Suddenly thinking.)* Why don't you get a letter?

CIG. A letter? I've never had one. *(Goes to chair, kneels on it, hands on back.)*

RAKE. Yes, a letter from some Johnny.

CIG. What's that?

RAKE. Well, that's just some man that admires you.

CIG. Even if I did, I couldn't read it.

RAKE. Bless your little heart. *(He kisses the tip of her nose.)* You see, that's the point—get him to read it to you. Let him read the letter!

CIG. Oh, you dear man! *(She embraces him.)* Sit down and write it. *(She places him in chair R. of table, pulls up chair and sits, pipe in hand.)* Write something that will burn into his very soul.

RAKE *(sits and takes up pen)*. Burn in his soul—burn in his soul. Ah—I have it! *(Writes.)* "My dear Cigarette"—*(Pause.)*

CIG *(takes lock of hair and brings it down around her nose, twirls end of it)*. That won't burn him.

RAKE. Won't it? *(Writes again.)* "My own little girl"—

CIG. Say, that's all right—and—queen of my heart. *(Stands on knees in her chair.)*

RAKE. Don't you think that's a little ordinary?

CIG. The witch doctress uses it. *(Leans over table close to him as he writes.)*

RAKE. All right. *(Writes.)* "I love you." *(Kisses her cheek.)*—And it's true. *(Very quietly.)*

CIG *(not noticing. He returns to writing as she dictates)*. "You are the sweetest girl in camp." No, "on earth." "On earth" sounds better.

"Sounds better" is not part of the letter. "You are the sweetest girl on earth. I will wait for you tonight."

RAKE *(she has dictated too fast for him to keep up with her).* Wait for me now. *(He writes very fast.)*

CIG. Say, Rake, where will he wait for me?

RAKE *(writing).* I don't know.

CIG. At the Moorish ruins, of course.

RAKE *(writing).* Rather damp amongst the ruins.

CIG. We will exchange vows.

RAKE. Good—very good.

CIG. That will scorch him. I think that is good enough to write twice.

RAKE. All right. *(Goes on writing.)*

CIG. No, scratch it out—it will take too long.

RAKE. Scratch out twice.

CIG. Yes. Now sign.

RAKE. Sign—sign what?

CIG. Rake—that's your name, isn't it?

RAKE. Yes, but Corporal Victor might object you know—

CIG. Well, then sign it—well, sign it—Adamond—

RAKE. Adamond.

(BERT calls outside. RAKE quickly folds the letter and gives it to CIGARETTE. He makes a quick exit into kitchen. BERT enters.)

BERT. Rake—Rake—

(CIGARETTE stands in center of room, letter over her heart.)
What's the matter, little girl?

CIG *(comes to him, points to letter).* It's a letter. *(She puts letter in his face.)*

BERT. So I see.

CIG. It's my first one—and I—I can't read it.

BERT. Your parents ought to have been whipped not to teach you.

CIG. Don't say that. My mother was a camp follower. Years ago the Bedouins captured her.

BERT. I'm sorry—

CIG. They tortured her and tossed her from one drunken devil to another, then cut her throat. I swore then to kill and kill and kill and I have kept my word.

BERT. And your father?

CIG. Who knows? After my mother was taken, my soldiers brought me up. But here—read the letter.

BERT *(reads).* "My own little girl."

(CIGARETTE shows joy at the success of her plan.)
Shall I go on?

(She nods.)
"Queen of my heart, I love you. You are the sweetest girl in camp, on earth sounds better."

(CIGARETTE starts as he reads this, then knowing it is RAKE's fault,

she shakes her fist at the door. BERT *does not see this. When he looks at her, she composes her face.)*
(Resumes reading). "I will wait for you tonight at the Moorish ruins, rather damp among the ruins."
(He laughs. She stamps her foot and mumbles cuss words.)
"Twice—scratched—Adamond." *(He rises.)*
CIG *(goes to him and snatches letter).* You're not jealous?
BERT. Jealous?
CIG. Yes, that's what I said.
BERT. Of who, Adamond?
CIG. No, of Rake, your skinny, stupid friend. He wrote the letter. *(Tears it up and jumps on it.)*
BERT. Why, little girl, I'm heartbroken. Why didn't you warn me?
CIG. Because I wanted to see if Entamaboull spoke the truth.
BERT. What did he say?
CIG. He said that when you got tired of me, you would throw me out the window.
BERT. I'll knock his head off for that.
CIG. Then it isn't true?
BERT. Why, it's absurd.
CIG. Then there's no other woman?
BERT. Nonsense. *(Turns away.)*
CIG *(looking at him. He has turned his back, knowing that he is deceiving her. She stamps foot.)* Then I suppose you won't be hurt by what I've got to say about her.
BERT *(turning quickly).* About who?
CIG. About the Lady Venetia.
BERT. Venetia?
CIG. Yes, the woman Bert loved.
BERT. Where did you hear this?
CIG. I heard it from the Zouaves.
BERT. It's a lie! I'll call them out singly or six at a time to extermi-nate the whole brigade.
CIG. We're quits—quits—quits! I knew nothing. I picked up two names by chance. I fired in the air and the bullet went straight to your heart. *(Goes to door, stands looking off.)*
BERT. Little one, I know I'm a fool to behave like this, but if you only knew—if you only knew.
CIG. I know now—I do know. You told me you loved me, but you still love her! *(Stamps foot and exits.)*
BERT. Cigarette, wait—Cigarette! *(He follows her off.)*
(Enter ROCKINGHAM *with champagne. He takes it to table, brings glasses, has back to entrance when* VENETIA *enters. She is wearing soft, light dress, appropriate to the hot North African climate.)*
VENETIA. Pardon me, sir, but could you direct me to—
ROCK *(turns and sees her).* My God, Venetia, what are you doing here?

VENETIA. I was touring the Moorish ruins and lost my way. What are you doing in that uniform?

ROCK. Exactly what you would assume.

VENETIA. There was such talk after you disappeared. No one knew where you went—such guesses, such gossip. And Bert, what about Bert?

ROCK. Beg your pardon.

VENETIA. Bert Cecil—you know whom I speak of.

ROCK. Oh yes, dear old Bertie. I heard that, like me, he lost all his money. I wonder what became of him.

VENETIA. Don't you know?

ROCK. I suppose he went to the Klondike—America—or some other place.

VENETIA. When I saw you, I had hopes of seeing him again.

ROCK. I can't quite see why you should. But what brings you to Africa?

VENETIA. Our future was in danger. The old Duke's will provided that my husband must serve with the Legion, as the family has for generations.

ROCK. And Chateauroy consented to that?

VENETIA. He had no choice. He has just been appointed Colonel of the Chasseurs.

ROCK. Of the Chasseurs? Chateauroy—our Colonel?

VENETIA. Tell me honestly, do you know where Bert Cecil is?

ROCK. Come, Venetia, your husband will be missing you. Go to this next corner and ask the guard on duty there to take you to your hotel.

(CIGARETTE is heard singing off.)

Quick, someone is coming. You can't be seen here in this wine shop. Go in there.

(He pushes her behind curtain. Enter BERT.)

BERT. What is the matter with you?

ROCK. I had a sunstroke.

BERT. Well, you're as pale as if you'd seen a ghost.

ROCK. It's nothing—I'll be all right.

(Enter RAKE.)

RAKE. It's a woman. *(Pulls up curtain, revealing VENETIA's skirt.)* Jack's got a woman.

BERT. Jack, why didn't you tell us?

(All laugh. VENETIA re-enters.)

ROCK. The jig is up. Come, Rake.

(They exit.)

BERT. Venetia, my God!

VENETIA. Are you afraid? Why do you turn from me?

BERT. Why have you come here?

CIG *(enters D.R.).* The Silver Pheasant! *(Exits D.R.)*

VENETIA. I have come with my husband. He could no longer avoid serving his time with the Legion and retain his fortune. He has just been made Colonel of the Chasseurs.

A chastened and penitent Venetia pleads with her former suitor to forgive her mistake. Venetia is now the wife of the Marquis de Chateauroy, who has been appointed Colonel of the Chasseurs in North Africa. Kathleen Murphy as Venetia, Richard Rorke as Bert Cecil.

BERT. The Chasseurs!

VENETIA. Oh Bert, he has made my life a nightmare. No sooner were we married than he began to torture me. You knew—you knew him. Why didn't you tell me?

BERT. You knew he was a gambler and a cheat. You knew it that night when I threw the cards in his face.

VENETIA. But he convinced us all that the charge was false.

BERT. Oh, easily, no doubt.

VENETIA. Some say I only got my just desserts, but if you only knew—

BERT. Venetia—I have tried to forget you. Let me. Through these past two years, the bivouac, the campfire, and the heat of battle— your face was always before me. At first, my only wish was that an Arab's spear would put an end to my life and I might die with your name upon my lips.

VENETIA. But now fate has brought us together again.

BERT. A fate I never should have wished for. *(Goes to her, embraces her.)* Venetia, you can't draw back now.

VENETIA. When shall it be?

(Noise outside. Enter soldiers, RAKE, ROCKINGHAM, *girls.)*

ENTAMABOULL. Wine! We want wine! Music!

(General movement; men pour drinks, girls bring wine to them; there is loud conversation.)

BERT *(aside to* VENETIA*).* Tomorrow night then.

VENETIA. At the Villa Aiyussa, at ten.

BERT. I will be there.

VENETIA. Don't disappoint me. Don't make me repent.

(Embrace and she exits. CIGARETTE *enters.)*

CIG *(aside).* Oh, God help me.

*(*CIGARETTE *looks at* BERT. *He retires and looks off as if watching.* CIGARETTE *takes off her uniform coat, goes C. and begins dance.* The girls join her. At the beginning of the dance,* PAULETTE *gets up and goes to chair at R. of table and stands on it.* BOUAMANA *goes D.R. to* BEAU, YUSSEF *and* TIGER CLAW. *The dance becomes more and more desperate and frantic. All clap for* CIGARETTE *as she dances. She dances to* BERT, *who each time turns away. At the last of the dance, she throws her canteen to* ENTAMABOULL, *and then falls exhausted in a faint.)*

CURTAIN

*Music for CIGARETTE's *Dance on page 159.*

SCENE TWO

SCENE: *Ace of Spades, the following morning. Discovered are* ROCKINGHAM *and* RAKE. RAKE *is at couch,* ROCKINGHAM *pacing.*

RAKE. I tell you, Cap'n, you might as well save your shoe leather. There's nothing we can do.

ROCK. There is—there has to be. Why, if Chateauroy should get wind of this—

RAKE. Well, what could he do? All three of us got our discharges and we're out of it all tomorrow.

ROCK. Yes, out of the Legion, but I'd sooner go through Zeralia again than see Bert go back to Venetia.

RAKE. Well, there's no accountin' for tastes, as they say. As for me, I wouldn't put all the titles in the Empire up against that little girl. *(Gestures* D.R. *to indicate* CIGARETTE *is inside.)*

ROCK. Nor I. Well, at any rate, it's luck we had our papers signed before Chateauroy took command. If it had been left to him, we'd all be turned down.

RAKE. And sent to Timbuktu in the bargain, I'll wager.

ROCK. I know it's not our business, but we've got to talk to him. We must get some sense into his head.

RAKE. Then you'll have to do it. I never could.

(Enter TIGER CLAW, ENTAMABOULL, YUSSEF, *and* BEAU BRUNO.*)*

ROCK. Come along— I think we'll find him at the barracks—at least we'll try. *(Exit.)*

TIGER. So, our brave vivandiere fights Bedouins and kills like a tiger, but faints for love.

ENTA. Ah, he will soon tire of her and she will be back with us where she belongs.

YUSSEF. Tell me where all of you would be if it were not for Cigarette. Many's the time she's slashed us all out of a tight spot when we would have been killed or captured.

TIGER. The Bedouins say she's a witch.

BEAU. And well she may be, the way she rides into battle and comes out without a scratch.

(Enter CHATEAUROY, *in Colonel's uniform. The soldiers all rise to attention.)*

CHAT. as you were. Gentlemen, I am your new commander, Colonel Chateauroy, Chasseurs D'Afrique. I am searching for a young woman, whose bravery, I understand, turned the tide of battle at Zeralia.

YUSSEF. It did, sir. Two companies sprang at her bidding from the ground and turned defeat into victory.

BEAU. And on Columbus sands, she rode into battle with a raven on her shoulder and scattered the enemy like a mist.

CHAT. Who is this woman? I was told I might find her here.

(Enter CIGARETTE *with wine jug.)*

YUSSEF. Here she is—Cigarette—the bravest soldier in all Africa!

CIG *(puts wine jug on table, salutes)*. Colonel?

CHAT *(to soldiers)*. I would speak with this young woman alone.

(Soldiers exit hurriedly.)

I am Colonel Chateauroy, newly in command of the Chasseurs D'-Afrique. I have heard of your bravery since my arrival here two days ago and have come to offer my compliments and your country's gratitude. *(Offers medal.)*

CIG. I've had enough of medals, thanks.

CHAT. And, upon meeting you, I'd like to add that you're a very pretty girl.

CIG. Ah, sir, your compliments and interest please me, but I would ask a favor.

CHAT. Anything you wish, provided it is within my power.

CIG. I want one of your corporals locked in the guardhouse overnight.

CHAT. What? Have one of my men locked in the guardhouse to please a minx? Well, this is delicious. And what will you give me if I do?

CIG. My friendship—that's all—will you do it?

CHAT. He must be a very foolish man to earn the displeasure of Cigarette. What's his name?

CIG. Corporal Victor.

CHAT. What regiment?

CIG. Chasseurs D'Afrique.

CHAT. And what has he done?

CIG. He's tired of me.

CHAT. He's an idiot. *(He moves toward her.)*

CIG *(moving back)*. He wants to throw me out the window.

CHAT. I'll catch you. *(He moves to embrace her. She slips out of reach.)*

CIG. He met the woman he loved in former years.

CHAT. They have a way of turning up.

CIG *(mockingly)*. And hoped he might die with her name on his lips.

CHAT. How romantic.

CIG. I must prevent their meeting.

CHAT. They have arranged one?

CIG. Yes—on the Blidah road tonight—at ten.

CHAT. And where is the rendezvous to be?

CIG. The Villa Aiyussa.

CHAT. The Villa Aiyussa! And who is the woman, do you know?

CIG. I call her "The Silver Pheasant." Her name is Lady Venetia.

CHAT *(aside)*. My wife! *(Aloud.)* And the man—what was his name before?

CIG. He was Bert Cecil.

CHAT. Where can I find him?

CIG. I know a tumble-down shack in the Moorish ruins. I could bring him there.

CHAT. No, it would be best to take him red-handed at the Villa Aiyussa. *(Calls out.)* Sergeant!

(Enter ENTAMABOULL.*)*

Meet me at the Villa Aiyussa at nine tonight.

ENTA. Yes, Colonel. *(Exits.)*

CIG. You won't hurt him? No blows—no wounds—injuries?

CHAT. Well, my girl, I thought you wanted revenge. Very well, only enough persuasion to bring him into the guardhouse.

CIG. And will you turn him loose in the morning?

CHAT. Yes, and I shall bring him back to you myself—humble and penitent. *(Exit.)*

CIG. Ha-ha-ha, Master Victor. It isn't wise to fool with Cigarette!

CURTAIN

SCENE THREE

SCENE: *Wine Shop that evening. At rise,* RAKE *and* ROCKINGHAM *are at table playing cards.* YUSSEF *is at back of table, looking on.*

ROCK. There, that's the fourth game tonight. You're careless.

(Enter BERT.*)*

Bert, take his hand.

*(*RAKE *rises and goes to window.)*

BERT *(pours drink).* No—I can't—I'll be going out soon.

ROCK. Is it a girl?

BERT. Yes.

ROCK. What kind of girl?

BERT. A female girl.

ROCK. Well, if you're going to meet Venetia—

BERT. Well, what if I am?

ROCK. Just this. You ought to be kicked from here to the Sahara, and if Chateauroy doesn't do it—

BERT. I've had enough of your good advice.

ROCK. Now see here, Bert, Chateauroy is a low-down blackguard, we both know that, but Venetia married him with her eyes wide open.

BERT. Jack—he has made the poor girl's life a hell. This is her only chance to escape from it, and I'm going to give it to her.

ROCK. Well, she can go anywhere she likes and take anything she wants, so long as she doesn't take you. Bert—it's Cigarette—I won't let you break her heart.

BERT. Ah, she'll soon forget. I'm not the only one and there'll be others.

RAKE. Master Cecil, sir, ever since you took me out of jail, I've been as true to you as a blooming shadow, but if you do this thing, I'll jolly well let you go to the devil in your own way.

ROCK. Those are my sentiments.

(RAKE comes to him. They shake hands silently.)

Good—good.

(RAKE retires to window. Enter CIGARETTE.)

CIG. Ah, you're all here. Yussef, my keg.

(Takes off wineskin and throws it to YUSSEF, who exits.)

As the cards are out and the whiskey here—

ROCK. I'm very sorry, Cigarette, but I promised to pitch quoits with Tiger. *(Goes to door, looks at BERT who is at the table, turns to CIGARETTE and puts his arms around her.)* Cigarette, do you know, you're a damn fine little girl. *(He circles to door. Aside.)* I'll pitch those quoits at the Villa Aiyussa. *(Exits.)*

CIG. You won't desert me, Rake?

RAKE *(getting up and going to door)*. I must, Cigarette, I have to go and plant—well—I'm going to plant a banana tree. *(Aside.)* I'll plant it at the Villa Aiyussa. *(Exits.)*

BERT. Little woman, I've a confession to make.

CIG. I know—you're going to meet the Lady Venetia at the Villa Aiyussa at ten tonight.

BERT. How did you know that?

CIG. Oh, a convenient curtain—I heard it all.

BERT. Did you tell anyone?

CIG. Would it interest anyone?

BERT. No, I don't think it would.

CIG. She still loves you and you love her; why do you deny it? *(Goes to window at back.)* It's nights like this that bring back all the memories—nights in the desert seated on a rug outside your tent—

BERT. I've told you, Cigarette—it's over for both of us.

CIG. Yes, I know how foolish I am. I keep thinking you care. You didn't even ask me of my adventures on the sands this afternoon.

BERT. What happened? Were you hurt?

CIG. Nothing hurts me—not even being jilted.

BERT. Stop it, Cigarette. You promised we'd be friends.

CIG. Do you think I could share you?

BERT. Don't talk like this. It's all over between us. *(He starts out.)*

(CIGARETTE runs between him and door.)

CIG. No, you shan't go yet.

BERT. Don't try to stop me.

CIG. I mean—I mean—I don't want you to go yet. You have a whole hour. You will have plenty of time, and this is the last time I will ever see you. I'll have to give you up forever.

(She buries her face in her hands and sobs. He holds her.)

BERT. Cigarette, you can't do this. It's idiotic.

CIG. I know—I know—all love is idiotic, but I can't forget and I can't give you up. Remember that night on the desert—we were outside your tent, the regimental band was playing at the officer's quarters, not a cloud in the sky, your arms around me, music all around us, and you told me—you told me that you loved me!

BERT. Cigarette, believe me, whatever happens, I will never be that happy again.

CIG. I mustn't believe you again—yet I love to hear you say it! Say it, oh, say it again, please!

BERT. Little girl, when I first met you *(hands on her shoulders.)*, I had lost the woman I loved. I thought I'd had all the suffering a man could stand in his life, and living it was the same as being dead. It was you who brought me back again—you who taught me it was better to go on with the fight than run amuck on an Arab bullet.

CIG. And you would leave me now? You can't—you won't leave me to go back to the old rut. Oh, I was happy enough till you came. I knew nothing of life but the dancing, the Zouaves, and the rough men who are my soldiers. *(She goes to him, pleading.)* But now they sicken me. I want to get away—to live like you want me to. I can do better, I know I can. Help me—don't leave me! *(Falls at his feet weeping.)*

BERT *(raises her up, arms around her, kisses her tears).* I won't, little one, I won't. I didn't lie to you—God help me, Cigarette, I love you.

CIG. You mean it now, don't you? Oh, I'm so happy I can't believe it! Write to the silver pheasant and tell her. Rake will take the letter and tonight we'll march down to the barracks before them all. *(She dries her eyes, straightens her hair.)* Fall in.

(BERT stands at attention.)

Forward march!

BERT *(comes down in marching order).* Halt, eyes front!

(Both click heels and face front.)

CIG *(salutes).* Corporal Victor.

BERT *(salutes).* Full Private Cigarette.

CIG. Friends, comrades in arms. *(Runs to him.)* Lovers forever!

(They embrace. CIGARETTE starts to door, turns and runs springing into his arms, arms about him. Then she runs off and is heard singing off.)

BERT. Sing on, little woman, sing on. I've been a fool, but I'm a fool no longer. I'll write to Venetia and tell her and then I'll be free again, free as I've only been free with Cigarette. *(Sits and starts to write.)* No, I mustn't write and I mustn't send Rake. I'll go myself.

(Enter YUSSEF, who hangs barrel on nail and stands at door.)

Yes, I'll go to the Villa Aiyussa. *(Takes hat and exits.)*

YUSSEF. The Villa Aiyussa. *(Exits.)*

(Enter CIGARETTE.)

CIG. Now to pluck the feathers from The Silver Pheasant, and we'll do it too, won't we, Victor? *(Looks around and, not seeing him, exclaims.)* Where is he? Oh—why should he frighten me like this?

(Runs to door and looks out, then to window and back.) Could he have gone? No, I won't believe it. Victor—Victor! *(Calls out door.)*

(Enter YUSSEF.*)*

Where is Corporal Victor, Yussef? Where is he?

YUSSEF. Oh, mistress, he took his hat and went—

CIG. Where—where did he go? *(Goes to* YUSSEF *and catches him by the throat as though to choke the answer out of him.)* Answer me—where did he go?

YUSSEF. I heard him say—

CIG. What?

YUSSEF. I will go—

CIG. Where?

YUSSEF. Oh, mistress, he said to the Villa Aiyussa. *(She releases him.)*

CIG. To the Villa Aiyussa!

(Exit YUSSEF.*)*

To her—to The Silver Pheasant—after all he said to me. It was all a lie, a lie, a lie. Oh, he shall have company, more company than he ever expected. Liar! Liar! Liar! *(Exit, sobbing hysterically.)*

CURTAIN

ACT THREE

SCENE ONE

SCENE: *The Villa Aiyussa, in the garden of the desert villa. Lights down. Moon effect on water at back. Curtained doors under portico. U.R. Enter* CHATEAUROY, *followed by* ENTAMABOULL. CHATEAUROY *comes downstage, goes C. and looks off.*

CHAT. Stand by orders.

ENTA. Yes, my Colonel. *(Salutes.)*

CHAT *(looks at curtain door, peeps in, but does not disturb curtain more than is absolutely necessary).* Place a sentry at the door of the courtyard. Let anyone in, but challenge all who go out. Sergeant, you have nothing to do with this man's innocence or guilt.

ENTA. No, my Colonel. *(Salutes.)*

CHAT. I'll see to your advancement.

ENTA. Thanks, my Colonel. *(Salutes.)*

CHAT. Now, follow me.

(He exits R. ENTAMABOULL *follows. After a pause,* RAKE *peeps on, then disappears. The same business is repeated, and then he enters, looks around, and motions to someone outside. He stands at attention, while* ROCKINGHAM *enters slowly.* RAKE *salutes.* ROCKINGHAM *nods his head indicating the door which is curtained.* RAKE *salutes and goes to curtain, taps on door, returns C.* ROCKINGHAM *retires up a little. Enter* VENETIA *from curtained door. She is dressed in a full-length negligee, her hair loose over her shoulders, tied with a ribbon.)*

VENETIA. Bert—I—I—Rockingham!

ROCK. Yes—and as there's little time to lose, and I've no aspirations to join the heavenly choir, I'll get to the point. Venetia, your conduct won't wash.

VENETIA. And by what right do you judge my conduct?

ROCK. By my friendship for Bert and my fondness for cards. We had a little whist party, which you interrupted.

RAKE. And the jolliest little whist party, if you please, my lady.

ROCK. Scoot, Rake, I think I can handle this better alone.

RAKE. Yes, sir. *(Salutes and exits.)*

ROCK. A whist party, where the cordiality of the players compensated for the smallness of the stakes.

VENETIA. What is that to me?

ROCK. Just this. I don't propose to have it broken up. Bert has other interests now, and I'm going to prevent his running away with you, if I'm compelled to blow the top of his head off in the process.

VENETIA. How did you know?

ROCK. Never mind. Forewarned, forearmed. *(Exits, very slowly.)*

VENETIA. Other ties, other interests, he said. What can he mean? What if he is deceiving me? I can't believe it. I mustn't believe it. I'll force him to tell me the truth.

(Enter BERT. VENETIA *is downstage, she hears him, but does not turn.)*

BERT *(goes to her, extending hands).* Venetia—*(She remains motionless.)* have I offended you?

VENETIA. No, but I want to be perfectly frank with you. When we met in the wine shop, I was willing to follow you anywhere.

BERT. Well?

VENETIA. After coming here, I began to count the cost. I thought of the world's opinion, and I find I lack the courage to brave it.

BERT. Venetia, you have lifted a world of care from my conscience.

VENETIA. How is that?

BERT. Oh, I know I'd be a coward to carry out the plans we laid in the wine shop.

VENETIA. Have you relapsed into the gallantry of other days? Have you found another Guenevere or an Algerian Zu-Zu?

BERT. Not that, I swear, but for tonight enough that our senses are restored to us. Venetia, our love has never brought anything but misery to our lives. I wish—oh, God, how I wish—

VENETIA. Wish nothing.

BERT. Yes, I wish one thing. I wish that this hell, which is only a half step from heaven, may never come to us again. *(Extends hand.)* Goodbye.

(She remains motionless. BERT *exits hurriedly.)*

VENETIA. It's true—it's true, but who's the woman?

(Enter CIGARETTE *from over the balustrade.)*

Who's this?

CIG. Cigarette. *(Has pistol in belt; her hand is on it.)*

VENETIA. Come nearer, have no fear.

CIG. Fear? What fear have I of you, a bird of paradise that does nothing but spread its wings in the sun.

VENETIA. Why have you come here?

CIG. For two reasons: One is because I want to look at your clothes. *(She does so.)* They aren't like anything I've seen before. And the other is because I want to hurt you. *(Goes to her, puts up hands as if about to attack by taking her by the throat.)* If only I knew how. *(Retires back a step.)* All right, now that I've seen you—and although I hate you—I can't help saying that you are beautiful—very beautiful. I don't wonder men fall in love with you.

VENETIA *(taking a few steps forward).* What have I done?

CIG. You have stolen my Corporal.

VENETIA. Corporal?

CIG. Corporal Victor of the Chasseurs. *(She stands very straight.)*

VENETIA. The name is familiar.

CIG. Aye, you know him, you cannot deny it—Bert. *(She turns to* VENETIA.*)*

VENETIA *(starts).* Cecil.

CIG. Yes, until you slipped into the wine shop and saw him, he never looked at any girl but me—me—do you hear?

VENETIA. Then we are rivals?

CIG. Yes—yes.

VENETIA. I, daughter of the Lyonnesses of England.

CIG. And I—a soldier of France. *(Salutes.)*

VENETIA. Before so formidable a rival I must retire, but first let me tell you, your Corporal was here and went away.

CIG. Where do you meet next time?

VENETIA. Nowhere. We quarreled; is that not enough?

CIG. What did you quarrel about?

VENETIA. He had other ties.

CIG. Meaning me.

VENETIA. And as I had ties of my own—

CIG. What ties? *(Half turns to* VENETIA.*)*

VENETIA. Only a husband.

CIG. Husband? Who is he?

VENETIA. The Marquis of Chateauroy, Colonel of the Chasseurs— Good night. *(Exits into curtained room.)*

CIG. Chateauroy, Chateauroy—what have I done? *(Thoroughly frightened.)* Victor—he must be warned in time.

*(*BERT *enters R.* CIGARETTE *sees him, but he does not see her.)*

BERT. Strange. The sentry at the door of the courtyard asked me for the word, but I could not give it to him. *(Turns and sees* CIGARETTE.*)* Cigarette, you here?

CIG. Yes, but what—what is the matter?

BERT. It looks devilishly like a trap.

CIG. But who would betray you?

BERT. Why no one, but—*(Notices that* CIGARETTE *looks confused. He pushes her roughly.)* You? This is your loyalty—your love—you who would fight like a lion? You are a traitoress.

CIG. Victor, for God's sake, not that—not that. I did not know. I did not know that he was her husband. So help me, I did not know.

BERT *(embracing her).* There, there, it is all right.

CIG. And you forgive me?

BERT. There is nothing to forgive.

CIG. But the Black Hawk will accuse you.

BERT. He'll do that soon enough.

(A shot is heard offstage. ROCKINGHAM *and* RAKE *run on.* VENETIA *enters from curtained door.)*

CIG. Go in there, quick. *(Pointing to curtained door.)*

BERT. No, I'm not built that way.

CIG. Don't you see—remorse will kill me. Go, go—for God's sake— for my sake!

(Enter CHATEAUROY. BERT *goes in curtained door.)*

CHAT. What's this?

ROCK. Probably you don't remember me: Lord Rockingham, calling on the Lady Venetia.

CHAT. I don't remember you. *(To* VENETIA.*)* May I ask why you permit this rabble in my house?

VENETIA. There is no rabble.

CHAT. Do you wish me to tell you what I have to say?

RAKE *(starts to go)*. A family difference.

VENETIA. Rockingham.

CHAT *(to VENETIA)*. Where is your lover?

VENETIA. I need not reply to an insult.

CHAT. Where have you hidden him?

VENETIA. I have nothing to say.

CHAT. Then I must appeal to the informer. *(Pointing to CIGARETTE.)*

CIG *(coming down)*. That's all right. *(Salutes.)* Sir, I told you to lock Victor in the guardhouse over night. That's Cecil—because I thought he was in love with the silver pheasant—that's your wife. But I was wrong. He told me so on the way to the barracks, and he is in the barracks now.

CHAT *(to VENETIA)*. Do you confirm this story?

VENETIA. I do.

CHAT. And you, who I take is this fellow's friend?

RAKE *(salutes)*. The story is true.

ROCK. It is, sir.

CHAT. I regret to lay aside such a notable body of evidence, but I believe the girl is lying and it is my intention to have her flogged— flogged until she confesses the hiding place of her lover.

CIG. I'll see you in hell—

CHAT. Enough! *(Goes up.)* Guard!

(Enter ENTAMABOULL, with whip.)

Strip the girl!

ROCK. Chateauroy!

CHAT. Silence!

(ENTAMABOULL comes to CIGARETTE and takes off her jacket.)

Whip her until she confesses the trick she played on me, and I will send her paramour to the barracks. I'll have you treated for what you are, the lowest of camp followers!

(BERT comes from behind the curtain in time to hear the last speech. He goes to CHATEAUROY and strikes him in the face, knocking him down.)

BERT. Coward!

CHAT *(rising)*. I'll have your life for this—I'll have you court-martialed!

BERT. Too late, Chateauroy. Our discharge took effect at noon to-day! Now it's man to man.

CHAT. Then man to man let it be! *(To VENETIA.)* To your room, Venetia! *(She leaves.)*

BERT. Come, Cigarette.

(He picks her up in his arms and they exit.)

BLACKOUT

SCENE TWO

SCENE: *The Ace of Spades Wine Shop the next morning.* RAKE *is alone onstage.*

RAKE. We've been together more than forty years and it don't seem a day too much. Well, I suppose they'll get married, settle down and be happy, God bless 'em.

(*Enter* ROCKINGHAM.)

ROCK. Ah, good morning, Rake.

RAKE. Good morning, where is Master Cecil?

ROCK. Hasn't he been here yet?

RAKE. No.

ROCK. Have you heard anything of the Lady Venetia?

RAKE. Yes, he sent her packing. She sailed on the Crocodile today at eight.

ROCK. Good riddance.

(*Enter* BERT.)

Ah, good morning, Bert, where have you been?

BERT. To the adjutants, getting our discharge papers. We are now three free men.

ROCK. What is the next move?

BERT. Well, the whole world is before us.

ROCK. And the little girl?

BERT. Well—I hadn't thought of that.

RAKE. Well, after you and the little girl have settled down—

BERT. I'm not sure about the settling down part.

ROCK. You wouldn't be such a scoundrel.

BERT. I want to do the right thing, but unfortunately—

ROCK. As sure as you are alive—

BERT. That's just it. In half an hour, I may cease to adorn this celestial sphere.

RAKE. What's that?

BERT. When my discharge was in my pocket, I went to the club. There was Chateauroy and when he saw me, he said, "Who let that fellow in? This club is for officers, not rankers." "Chateauroy," I said, "I'm no longer Corporal Victor La Farge of the Chasseurs D'Afrique, I am Bert Cecil, your cousin, and I have to tell you that you are a liar, a forger, and a thief," and with that, I chucked a brandy in his face.

RAKE. Bully for you, sir, bully for you.

BERT. Two officers of the Zouaves at once advanced to be my seconds. That shows you how much they hate him. The time and the place is to be named at ten.

ROCK. Chateauroy is the best shot in the army.

BERT. Can't help that.

RAKE. Never missed his mark, sir.

BERT. More's the pity.

RAKE (*looking off*). Ah, here she comes.

(CIGARETTE *enters.*)

CIG. My three comrades! Jack! *(Embraces* ROCKINGHAM *then goes to* RAKE *and embraces him.)* Rake! *(After this, she turns and extends hand to* BERT. *He goes to her and they embrace.)*

ROCK *(goes to door and seeing that* RAKE *is still standing looking at* CIGARETTE, *he calls to him softly.)* Rake.

> *(*RAKE *does not hear him.* ROCKINGHAM *goes to* RAKE *and touches him on the shoulder.* RAKE *starts and exits.* ROCKINGHAM *follows him.)*

CIG. How high does the goose hang now?

BERT. Well, at least I'm a free man once more.

CIG. Yes, free, and the "Silver Pheasant" has gone out of our lives forever. When you promised me, why didn't you keep your word?

BERT. I did. I went to her and told her everything.

CIG. Never mind. It's good to have you home again. Soon you will be quarreling with Jack in the same old way, and Rake will be trying to keep peace between you.

BERT. I'm afraid we won't quarrel here any more.

CIG. Why?

BERT. Jack, Rake and I have our walking papers. Look, little woman, I know what you've done for me, but suppose I were to drop out of sight—vanish?

CIG. I know—I know—the silver pheasant has gone, but she has taken your heart with her.

BERT. No—no.

CIG. Ah, you can't forgive me for betraying you—I can't forgive myself.

> *(Enter* RAKE, *hurriedly.)*

RAKE. Mr. Cecil, sir, Jack is bringing in a half-blind girl picked up on the desert who says she is looking for you.

BERT. Who is she?

RAKE. I think that—

> *(*RENEE *enters.* ROCKINGHAM *helps her.)*

BERT. Renee Baroni!

RENEE. I took passage to Algiers. There was a storm—they put me off at Samula—

BERT. Yes—yes—

RENEE *(growing weaker and confused).* I set out alone—wandered for days—lost in whirling sand—but now I've found you—I've come to tell you—

BERT. Yes, to tell me?

RENEE. That it was I who cheated you out of your fortune—forged your uncle's will.

BERT. Impossible—you would never—

RENEE. Baroni forced me. But now he's dead and can never torture me again!

ROCK. Poor girl!

RENEE. The proof is here. *(Reaches inside cloak and brings out papers.)*

ROCK *(looking at papers).* The original will!

RAKE. Mr. Cecil, you will once more be Lord of Chateauroy Manor. Congratulations!

ROCK. Congratulations!

CIG *(aside).* Lord of Chateauroy Manor?

BERT. But why, Renee? Why would you come so far to find me?

RENEE. Because you are my—my—*(Faints on the end of the line.)*

BERT. Take her to the hotel. *(Picks her up and gives her to* ROCKINGHAM *who exits with her.)* When she is well, we'll take her back to Chateauroy Manor—

CIG. Chateauroy Manor?

RAKE *(quietly, to* BERT). The arrangements for the duel have been settled. Ten o'clock at the Moorish ruins. Good Luck, Mr. Cecil. *(Exits.)*

CIG. You will go back to Chateauroy Manor—and I? What would the ladies there think of me? I, who smoke, and sit on troopers' knees?

BERT. Cigarette, I'm called away, but in less than half an hour, I will return, and in the presence of everyone in that canteen, I will ask you to do me the honour of becoming my wife. *(Extends hand.)*

CIG. It's because you pity me. Don't speak—if it is not so, let me think you mean it just for a moment, Victor—Victor. *(Embrace.)*

RAKE *(enters).* All is ready, sir.

BERT. In a moment, Rake.

CIG. Goodbye—in half an hour.

BERT. Yes, even less. Goodbye.

(He kisses her and goes to door. RAKE *hands him a box.)*
Rake, keep her company until I return. *(Shakes hands with* RAKE *and exits.)*

RAKE. Ah, here we are, Cigarette. Here are some sandwiches we didn't finish. Come, let's have some lunch. *(Goes to shelf; takes down plate with bread and knife; goes to table and begins cutting it.)*

CIG. Rake, I feel as if I were going to cry.

RAKE. Cry? Pooh, pooh, I know a cure for that. There's a music hall song I used to sing. It goes—

(SONG: *"Underneath the Arches"**)

Underneath the arches, I dream my dreams away.
Underneath the arches, on cobblestones I lay.
Every night you'll find me, tired out and worn,
Happy when the daylight comes creeping, heralding the dawn.
Sleeping when it's raining, and sleeping when it's fine,
I hear the trains, rattling by above.
Pavement is my pillow, no matter where I stray,
Underneath the arches, I dream my dreams away.

*Music on page 155.

CIG. Rake, did you notice anything strange about Mr. Victor when he went away? Come to think of it, he kissed me as if he were going away forever.

RAKE. Nonsense! Now there's a ballad runs a trifle livelier. *(Sings.)* That's called "Lily of Laguna". *(He dances U.C.)*

(SONG: *"Lily of Laguna"* *)

She's my lady love,
She is my girl, my baby love,
She's the girl for sittin' down to drink,
She's the only girl Laguna knows

I know she likes me,
I know she likes me, because she said so,
She is my Lily of Laguna,
She is my Lily and my own.

CIG. Rake, you know where he has gone to?

RAKE. I—I—little girl—*(Backing away, more and more nervous; he takes out handkerchief.)*

CIG *(pressing him)*. Rake—you are nervous.

RAKE. I—I—I—

CIG. Yes, you are as nervous as I am.

RAKE *(aside)*. They should have met by this time.

CIG. Rake, there is something I have to tell you. I hardly dare tell. Victor promised to return in half an hour, to ask me to be his wife. His wife. *(Pause.)* Ah, you see the time is flying by. This absence isn't natural. *(She looks out.* RAKE *is by door.)* Rake—is that clock right?

RAKE. I think it is fast, Cigarette.

CIG *(looks around and notices that box is gone)*. His pistols are gone. He is fighting a duel!

RAKE. If you would know the truth, he had to clear the score.

CIG. With the Black Hawk whose aim means death! *(Starts to go.)*

RAKE *(trying to stop her)*. You mustn't go, Cigarette, you mustn't go!

CIG *(pushing him aside)*. Don't stop me—don't stop me! *(She exits and is heard calling in distance.)* Victor—Victor!

RAKE. I thought I liked the master pretty well, but before a love like that!

(Two shots heard, a short pause between them.)

It's over. *(Goes to window, looks out.)* There's a man running down the street. Can it be Cecil? *(Goes to door, opens it.)*

(ROCKINGHAM *runs in all out of breath.)*

ROCK. It's over, Rake.

RAKE. Was it Mr. Cecil?

ROCK. No.

Music on page 156.

RAKE. The Black Hawk, then?

ROCK (*quietly*). No.

RAKE. Then who? (*Pause.*) My God—not—not?

ROCK (*nods head*). Yes. They drew lots. Cecil won and fired first. Chateauroy was fatally winged, but the devil's luck was with him as he pressed the trigger. (*Slowly turns to face* RAKE.) The little girl threw herself on Bert and received the bullet in her heart.

> (*Enter* TIGER CLAW, BEAU BRUNO, ENTAMABOULL *and* YUSSEF *who arrange chairs for bed.* YUSSEF *gets D.R. chair and puts it in front of couch.* BERT *enters from U.R. carrying* CIGARETTE. *He puts her on couch as others close in.* ROCKINGHAM *is at foot of couch on one knee.* RAKE *stands behind* BERT, *the Arab soldiers are behind* RAKE *in a line.* BEAU *is at* CIGARETTE's *head. The Arabs stand to attention.*)

CIGARETTE (*rising on elbow*). Victor—Victor!

> (*He bends over her. She puts arm around him. He bows head.*)

Don't cry for me. It is better as it is. But I always loved you—ah, my soldiers, my soldiers.

> (ROCKINGHAM *and* RAKE *kneel in front of couch. Arabs do the same at back.*)

Think of me when I'm gone. Ah, Ma Belle, my flag!

> (RAKE *gets flag, hands it to* ROCKINGHAM, *who hands it to* CIGARETTE. ROCKINGHAM *holds staff.* CIGARETTE *wraps flag around her neck.*)

Let me have this when I am gone. (*Holds up one end of flag.*) Tell them in France I died for the flag. (*Becoming unconscious of her surroundings, as in a dream.*) The bugle is sounding for parade.

> (BERT *comes in front of couch.*)

I'll answer. Cigarette—child of the Army—soldier of France! (*Falls back dead.*)

> (*"La Marseillaise" plays softly.*)

BERT. Cigarette! (*Falls on knees and bows head, holding her hand.*) (*Arabs and* RAKE *salute.*)

CURTAIN

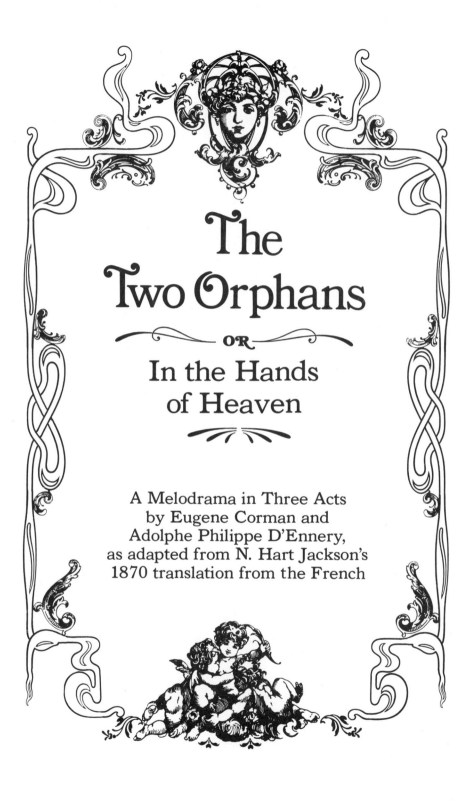

The
Two Orphans

OR

In the Hands
of Heaven

A Melodrama in Three Acts
by Eugene Corman and
Adolphe Philippe D'Ennery,
as adapted from N. Hart Jackson's
1870 translation from the French

CAST OF CHARACTERS

ANTOINE, in the service of the Marquis de Menton
PICARD, valet to De Vaudrey
JACQUES FROCHARD, from a line of outlaws
PIERRE FROCHARD, his brother
LA FROCHARD, mother of Jacques and Pierre
LOUISE, a blind orphan
HENRIETTE, also an orphan
JEANETTE, an outcast
BARON MAURICE DE VAUDREY, a young nobleman
COUNT EDMUND LEVANT, Minister of Police
COUNTESS DIANE LEVANT, his wife, her heart carries a guilty secret
DOCTOR, of the hospital and prison
SISTER GENEVIEVE, Sister Superior of the hospital
CLERK
POLICEMAN
MARIE MORAND, prisoner
JEANNE RAYMOND, prisoner

SYNOPSIS OF SCENES

Time: September 1865   Place: Paris

ACT ONE

Scene One: An open square near the Pont Neuf.
"You have fallen into good hands!"

Scene Two: Apartment of Baron De Vaudrey.
"Miserable scoundrel—give me room!"

ACT TWO

Scene One: Office of the Minister of Police.
"I defend your honor against yourself."

Scene Two: In front of the Church of St. Sulpice.
"Kill me, kill me if you like, but I love her."

Scene Three: Henriette's room.
"Take this girl to prison."

ACT THREE

Scene One: The prison courtyard.
                 "Punishment may purify a guilty soul."

Scene Two: The hut of La Frochard.
                 "The rest is in the hands of heaven."

Kate Claxton, shown here on her pallet of straw at the Frochards', eventually bought the rights to The Two Orphans *and toured with it for several years. Legend has it that she wore a small bag of ice suspended down her bosom for the snow scene, so that she might shiver and weep more realistically.*

PROGRAMME
UNION SQUARE THEATRE.

VOL. VI.   NEW YORK, WEDNESDAY, FEBRUARY 24, 1875.   No. 135.

Proprietor,- - - Mr. Sheridan Shook
Manager, - - - Mr. A. M. Palmer

This and every evening this week, and Saturday Matinee at 1.30 P.M., the Grand Romantic Drama in Four Acts and Seven Tableaux, by ADOLPHE D'ENNERY (author of "Don Omar de Lazan," &c., &c.) and EUGENE CORMON, adapted expressly for this Theatre by HART JACKSON, Esq., entitled

THE TWO ORPHANS,

with the following cast:

CHEVALIER MAURICE DE VAUDREY,   MR. CHARLES R. THORNE, JR
COUNT DE LINIERES, Minister of Police,   MR. JOHN PARSELLE
PICARD, Valet to the Chevalier,   MR. STUART ROBSON
JACQUES FROCHARD, an Outlaw,   MR. McKEE RANKIN
PIERRE FROCHARD, the cripple, his brother,   MR. F. F. MACKAY
MAR'UIS DE PRESLES,   MR. W. J. COGSWELL
LAFLEUR, in the service of the Marquis de Presles,   MR. H. W. MONTGOMERY
DOCTOR of the Hospitals St. Louis and La Salpêtrière,   MR. THOS. E. MORRIS
MARTIN, Citizen of Paris,   MR. LYSANDER THOMPSON
OFFICER OF THE GUARD,   MR. J. W. MATHEWS
CHIEF CLERK, in the Ministry of Police,   MR. W. H. WILDER
DE MAILLY,   MR. BOLTON
D'ESTREES,   MR. RAYNOR
ANTOINE,   MR. W. J. QUIGLEY
FOOTMAN,   MR. C. M. COLLINS
COUNTESS DIANE DE LINIERES,   MISS FANNY MORANT
LOUISE,   The Two Orphans   MISS KATE CLAXTON
HENRIETTE,   MISS KITTY BLANCHARD
MARIANNE, an Outcast,   MISS MAUDE GRANGER
LA FROCHARD, Mother of   MISS MARIE WILKINS
SISTER GENEVIEVE   MISS IDA VERNON
JULIE,   MISS ROBERTA NORWOOD
FLORETTE,   MISS KATE HOLLAND
CORA,   MISS CORA CASSIDAY
SISTER THERESE,   MISS HATTIE THORPE

Soldiers, Guards, Ladies and Gentlemen, Prisoners, Nuns, &c., &c.

SYNOPSIS OF SCENERY.

ACT I.—TABLEAU I.   The Place Pont Neuf.
    TABLEAU II.   Illuminated Garden and Terrace at Bel-Air, near Paris.
ACT II.—TABLEAU I.   Private office in the Hotel of the Minister of Police.
    TABLEAU II.   The Place St. Sulpice.
ACT III.—TABLEAU I.   Henriette's Chamber.
    TABLEAU II.   Courtyard of the Prison of La Salpêtrière.
ACT IV.—TABLEAU I.   Boat House on the Bank of the River Seine.

The Music incidental to the piece composed and arranged by MR. H. TISSINGTON.

During the evening the Orchestra will perform the following selections :

OVERTURE—FRANZ SCHUBERT, - - - - SUPPE
WALZER (New)—THEORIEN, - - - - STRAUSS
POLKA (first time)—IL STACCATO, - - - BONNISSEAU
(Solo for the Cornet.)
MEDITATION (first time)—FADED FLOWERS, - - LANGE
ROMANZA—MAGIC BELLS, - - - JUNGENAN
GALOP—MADISON AVENUE, - - - PENELOPE
FANTASIE—SHINING LIGHTS, - - - H. TISSINGTON
(Introducing the Popular Song, Silver Threads among the Gold. Solo for the Xylo Calme Piano.)

Treasurer - - - - - Mr. E. H. GOUGE
Stage Manager - - - - Mr. J. W. THORPE

The Scenes all designed and painted by   MR. RICHARD MARSTON
Music composed and arranged by   MR. H. TISSINGTON
Properties by   Mr. W. HENRY
Gas and Lights by   MR. CHARLES MURRAY
The whole production under the stage direction of   MR. JOHN PARSELLE

The costumes worn in this play, both by the Ladies and Gentlemen were made and designed by Mr. T. W. LANOUETTE, 830 Broadway.

SATURDAY, Feb. 27, 1.30 P.M., TENTH MATINEE OF THE TWO ORPHANS.

The Elegant Rustic Furniture used in this Play is from the Establishment of Messrs. Thonet Bros., Vienna, and 808 Broadway.

OPERA GLASSES TO HIRE IN THE LOBBY.

This Theatre will be perfumed every Friday Evening with THE CROWN PERFUMES, dispersed through OUTWATER'S EUREKA VAPORIZERS, from ATWOOD'S PHARMACY, 846 Broadway, adjoining Wallack's Theatre.

PIANOS USED IN THIS THEATRE ARE FROM THE WAREROOMS OF ALBERT WEBER.

The Church Organ used is from the Warerooms of Mason & Hamlin.

About the Play

The Two Orphans was once praised by New York theatre impresario Daniel Frohman as being "the perfect play." It is one of the best written, most played and most durable plays of the 19th Century. Authored by Eugene Corman and Adolphe Philippe d'Ennery, it opened at the Porte St. Martin of Paris in January of 1874. From there it went to London stages and later was adapted by N. Hart Jackson for presentation at A.M. Palmer's Union Square Theatre in New York. There, with Kate Claxton in the role of Louise, it had 180 performances in its initial run. The play proved so successful that Miss Claxton took it on tour throughout the United States for approximately four years. She eventually bought the rights and made it her personal vehicle.

A particularly successful engagement featured Alice Dunning Lingard and her sister-in-law, Dickie Lingard, as the sisters at the California Theatre in San Francisco, where it netted $11,000 in seven performances, a record for that theatre.

Alice Dunning Lingard, with her sister-in-law, Dickie Lingard, brought The Two Orphans *to San Francisco in 1875. Dickie was Henriette, Alice was Louise.*

James O'Neill, the famous Irish actor, made his New York acting debut playing Pierre. An important New York revival in 1926 starred Fay Bainter, Henrietta Crosman, Robert Loraine and Wilton Lackaye. In 1922, D.W. Griffith used the play for his memorable silent movie, *Orphans of the Storm*, starring Lillian and Dorothy Gish. (See illustration on page 15.)

Grace George and Margaret Illington played the sisters in a star-studded revival in New York in 1904. James O'Neill was also in the cast, as well as Clara Morris, one of Augustin Daly's famous stars, making her farewell stage appearance in this production.

ACT ONE

SCENE ONE

SCENE: *Open square in a quiet section of Paris.* ANTOINE *is discovered seated at table with drink. He is middle-aged, a servant to the Marquis de Menton, crafty and obsequious. He is well-dressed, trying to look like an ordinary businessman. He glances nervously at his watch and looks off.*

ANTOINE. I might have known better than to depend on that popinjay Picard to arrive on time! If he's not after his masters' wallets, it's his wenches, and between the two it's a marvel he ever keeps an appointment. Ah, but I had little choice at that—he's the one valet in Paris who's been gentleman to the new Prefect of Police and knows the secrets of every nobleman at court. There's no one else discreet enough to assist me in this affair.

(Enter PICARD, *hastily. He is a young man, charming, intelligent and witty. He is dressed as a valet, and he removes his hat and bows with elegance.)*

PICARD. Auguste Picard! Valet-de-chambre to the Baron De Vaudrey, present and at your service, sir!

ANTOINE. And about time! Did you receive my message?

PICARD. I did, but it wasn't simple to get away. I have such an odd new master. At this hour, you'd think he'd be playing piquet at the club or dawdling with some young damsel—ahhhh! He takes his evening pleasures as any young nobleman ought to do, but he's up at dawn and he works, he actually works! He sits down and he reads and he writes, just as though he were some lawyer's clerk. He thinks peasants and common people should have rights just as he. Sometimes he talks to me and says, "Picard, the day is fast approaching when there will be no titles and privileges for the nobility of France." Now, what do you say to that?

ANTOINE. Strange! Strange talk indeed!

PICARD. That's what I tell him, but come, you said in your note you wanted my help.

ANTOINE. I do! Your help to serve a nobleman whose tastes are more akin to yours, I'll wager. You see, the Marquis—

PICARD. Ah, yes. I have heard rumors that a certain house of pleasure lies at the edge of the city—

ANTOINE *(looking around)*. Hush, we must be discreet! The Marquis de Menton wishes Chateau du Bel Air to have only the reputation of serving the rather special needs of his friends at court—

PICARD. Most understandable! Admirable as well! The divertissements in the city are becoming more and more distasteful to young noblemen of taste.

ANTOINE. Exactly, and the new minister of police less and less understanding, so I've been told. So, the good Marquis is prepared to pay well to provide only the best for his guests. His salon boasts the fairest girls in France.

PICARD. Indeed! I understand.

ANTOINE. Modestly, Picard, I will admit to you, I Antoine, have occasionally assisted the Marquis. That is, previously, I have made some arrangements, and now there is another in prospect.

PICARD. A very special one, I suppose. And is the price good?

ANTOINE. You will be well paid for the little work you will do. Listen to me and don't interrupt. Time is growing short. The Marquis returned today from a visit to the country. On the road, his carriage passed a coach, in which he discovered a young treasure, a Normandy girl.

PICARD. Ah, one of those Normandy beauties! With caps six feet high, rosy cheeks and wooden shoes!

ANTOINE. You're at it again—remember she's for noblemen and not for you. Now listen: he made her acquaintance when the passengers alighted for refreshment. He discovered she was coming to Paris in company with her sister, where they have no relations, but have been recommended to the care of an old fellow whom they expect to meet on this spot.

PICARD. And what am I to do?

ANTOINE. Get the old fellow out of sight. Take him to a tavern and get him drunk. Tell him the coach has been delayed for two hours by an accident. When he is drunk enough, turn him over to the tavern keeper to be put to bed, and come back and help me. (Hands him money.) Here, that's enough for brandy and the barkeep, too.

PICARD. True. He may want bribing if he's to keep our friend out of sight. Now, when does the coach arrive?

ANTOINE (looking at watch). At six o'clock. (Points off.) There's the old fellow now. I'll wait for the coach inside and trust him to you. Go quickly. (Exits into cafe.)

PICARD. (SONG: "Gentleman's Gentleman"*)

> I'd rather be a gentleman's gentleman than a gentleman
>   on my own.
> I wouldn't want a title or a throne;
> Any time I'm feeling frivolous
> And amorous, too,
> I know lots of courtly ladies who
> Like my parlez vous;
> I couldn't count the no-account counts whose
>   countesses count on me instead,

*Music on pages 158–159.

I'm very careful not to lose my head;
And though they don't invite me over to dine,
I've got the key to the cellar where they store the wine,
I'm a gentleman's gentleman all the time.

I wouldn't care to be a marquis 'cause my life's a lark
    as it is,
What do I care about the social whirl?
If the duke can't do the duties that
The duchess requires,
I'm the guy the duchess calls to come
Over and light the fires,
I never mind when measuring suits or polishing boots
    or mending hose,
Where do you think I got this suit of clothes?
And if an English lord and lady pay a visit to Paree,
I can take the lady while the lord is taking tea,
I'd rather be
A gentleman's gentleman
Any time.

(PICARD *exits. Enter* LA FROCHARD *at rear. She is a woman in her early forties, street tough, but pretty. Her shabby dress is carefully planned to evoke sympathy. She goes to members of the audience and begs.*)

FRO. My good man, charity, if you please, for an old woman.

(FROCHARD *moves on down, muttering.*)

Mongrels! Pigs! Dogs! (*She assumes a pious whine, accosts someone else.*) Charity—charity for a helpless old woman with seven children at home!

(LA FROCHARD *continues on up and onto stage, muttering curses under her breath. At the same time,* PIERRE *enters at back with scissors grinding wheel. He is* LA FROCHARD's *younger son, a slight hunchback, who walks with a limp from an injury suffered as a child. His clothing is worn and shabby, but clean and neat. He crosses, puts down wheel.*)

PIERRE (*coming front*). Knives to mend—scissors to grind! (*Sees* LA FROCHARD.) Why, mother, is that you?

FRO. Yes, it's me. You lazy good-for-nothing!

PIERRE. Lazy? Why, mother, I do all the work I can!

FRO. Work? You call that work? Bah! Why did Heaven bless you with such an ugly face—such a beautiful deformity? Why, to earn your living by, you puny thing—and you work, when all you need to do is to limp, hold out your hand, and make your fortune with your ugliness.

PIERRE. Mother, I cannot beg. It is not possible.

FRO. Eh? Not possible, why not?

PIERRE. Mother, when I was an infant you carried me through the streets and taught me begging prayers I did not understand. They put money into your pocket and I knew no shame. But now it is different. You drove me out and bade me come here to beg. But when I knelt and held out my hand to ask alms, shame choked me, and I was overcome by anger at my own humiliation. No mother, I cannot beg—I cannot!

FRO. Undutiful son, you would rather leave your poor brother and me to starve.

PIERRE. My brother need not starve; he has health and strength and you support him in idleness.

FRO. Why should my beautiful Jacques work? My handsome boy, the very image of his poor dead father, that those scoundrels of the law robbed me of.

PIERRE. Our father suffered death for a murder of which they found him guilty.

FRO. And can I look to you to avenge him? No, no, my handsome Jacques will do that. He's no milksop, nothing frightens him!

PIERRE. No, not even the sight of blood.

FRO. Shut up! You are good for nothing but to be honest. I hate honest people, scum that imposes on the poor. *(She comes down to audience.)* Good people, charity, for the love of Heaven!

PIERRE. Perhaps she is right, I am good for nothing except to be honest. Alas, I never had any one to teach me. *(Returns to his wheel, starts away with it, but stops as he hears noise in cafe.)* Ah!

(Laughter is heard in cafe. JACQUES *comes out. He is dark and handsome. In contrast to* PIERRE, *he is warmly dressed.)*

JACQUES. Hello! Here is the old woman and her precious abortion of a son. *(To* LA FROCHARD.*)* Has Jeanette come yet?

FRO. Not yet, my son.

JACQUES. Never mind, she'll come in time.

FRO. My son, do you need money? Or have you found a purse?

JACQUES. No, but Jeanette has. *(To* PIERRE.*)* Come here.

*(*PIERRE *comes down L.)*

FRO *(admiringly)*. Isn't he in a good humor?

JACQUES. Look ye! Good children always give an account of their earnings to their parents. Isn't that so, Mother?

FRO. Certainly, my lamb—you have excellent principles.

PIERRE. And when I give an account, you pocket it all.

JACQUES. Well, what if I do?

PIERRE. It is unjust—it is—

JACQUES *(threateningly)*. That's enough. None of your fine speeches. I want your money. How much have you got?

PIERRE *(hands the money to* LA FROCHARD*)*. Twenty-two livres, seven sous.

JACQUES *(taking money from* PIERRE's *hand)*. And all this fuss about that! Why, what have you been doing for a whole week?

PIERRE. I have walked the streets from morning until night, with my wheel upon my back. I have lived on bread and water. I could do no more.

JACQUES. Well, your trade don't pay. I must find you something better.

PIERRE. Something better? You? No! No! *(Returns to his wheel.)*

FRO. I have saved three livres, eighteen sous. Put them with Pierre's. That makes—

JACQUES. Oh, never mind how much it makes. I don't want it particularly, but I'll take it on principle. *(Takes money from LA FROCHARD.)* Come, cripple, let's drink.

PIERRE. No—I don't like to drink.

JACQUES. Why, who would think we are brothers? You have the blood of a sheep in your veins. You're a disgrace to the family. I boast the blood of a Frochard, the Frochards who have been outlaws for one hundred and fifty years.

FRO. Ah, what a man! I love him—he's so like his father.

JACQUES *(takes LA FROCHARD by the arm)*. Come along, then, if you love me. I'm thirsty. *(To PIERRE.)* Are you coming with us?

PIERRE. No, no, there's the Normandy coach has just arrived. I'll run and see if there's not a chance to earn a few sous.

(Coach horn and clatter of horses' hoofs off R. LA FROCHARD and JACQUES exit into cafe. Exit PIERRE R. ANTOINE comes out of cafe and watches as HENRIETTE and LOUISE enter; then he slowly wanders off without being noticed by them. HENRIETTE is a very pretty girl of about twenty, in peasant dress of the Normandy countryside. LOUISE is slightly smaller and younger; her dress is similar to HENRIETTE's but in different colors. She is obviously blind; she clings to HENRIETTE, who guides and cares for her. Both girls are dressed for travel. They wear gloves and carry suitcases.)

HENRIETTE *(comes to bench)*. Here, Louise, sit here!

LOUISE *(sitting)*. I am surprised that Monsieur Martin is not here to meet us!

HENRIETTE. Oh, he'll come soon! Ah, Louise, Paris is beautiful! My poor sister, if you could only see its wonders!

LOUISE. Tell me what you see! Where are we?

HENRIETTE. In an open square on the bank of a river and there's a beautiful bridge further down, which has a magnificent statue in the middle.

LOUISE. That's the Pont Neuf—papa used to speak of it!

HENRIETTE. And on this side I can see two great towers—it must be Notre Dame Cathedral.

LOUISE. Notre Dame. *(Sadly.)* How I wish I could see it. It was on that spot I, a helpless infant, was left to perish. There your dear father found me! But for him I should have died of cold and hunger—perhaps, perhaps that would have been better!

HENRIETTE. My darling sister, why do you say so?

LOUISE. I should not have lived to become blind and unhappy!

HENRIETTE. Louise, do not speak thus. Our dear parents loved us both alike. You were their consolation and happiness, and it was their first grief when Heaven deprived you of your sight.

LOUISE. Misfortune pursues me, sister. Scarcely had this affliction befallen me when we were left orphans and without help of friends.

HENRIETTE. No, no, dear Louise! Not without friends, I hope! I have turned all we possessed into money and have come to this great Paris, where there are skillful doctors who will soon restore my poor Louise's eyes to their old-time brightness! Come, do not be sad! Remember when we were little ones, remember how I could always comfort you when you were hurt—remember the happy tunes our dear father taught us to sing together?

(They sing, HENRIETTE leading off, LOUISE joining.)

HENRIETTE &
LOUISE   *(SONG: "If I Had a Wish"*)*

If I had a wish I'd wish for things,
No one ever thinks that wishing brings:
Something kind of odd, like a silver goldenrod
That would disappear when I nod.

If I had a wish, I'd wish to find,
Carved upon a tree with hearts entwined,
Names of all the beaus that the future holds
So that we could guess our betrothed.

Everyone wants to meet a wise man
Like the books reveal.
He would say magic words and then
Your wish would start being real.

If I had a wish I'd wish for you
Anything to make your wish come true.
What would be the fun when the wish were done
If it only came true for one.
If it only came true for one.

LOUISE. But where can Monsieur Martin be? Why doesn't he come for us?

HENRIETTE. Perhaps he is waiting in the cafe—I'll go in and see. *(Enters cafe, leaving LOUISE seated on bench.)*

(The voices of JACQUES and others are heard laughing boisterously in the cabaret. JEANETTE enters at back, pale and staggering. She is an outcast, a girl of the streets. She is young, but

*Music on page 157

shows signs of her difficult life. Her dress is gaudy but pretty, and she knows that she dresses to attract the attention of men.)

JEAN *(listens for a moment).* Yes, it is his voice, singing and laughing. Aye, drink and carouse. Forget her whose heart you have broken. Enjoy yourself while the victim of your brutality seeks the only refuge left to her—death! One plunge and it will all be over. *(She goes up to the quay.)*

(Re-enter HENRIETTE.*)*

May my dying shriek of despair ring in your ears as a never-ending curse! No, it is not yet dark enough. I might be seen and perhaps saved.

HENRIETTE *(to* LOUISE*).* He is not there!

LOUISE. And you do not see him here?

HENRIETTE *(anxiously looking around).* No, not yet. But what can be the matter with that woman? *(*JEANNETTE *falls.)* She has fallen; she must be ill.

LOUISE. Go to her! Speak to her, Henriette!

HENRIETTE *(going to* JEANETTE*).* Pardon me, madame; can I do anything for you?

JEAN. Nothing—nothing!

LOUISE *(to* HENRIETTE*).* She said that with a voice full of misery and despair.

HENRIETTE. Madame, have confidence in us. We are not rich, but if we can help you—

JEAN. I have already told you I want nothing and that I cannot be helped. There are griefs that cannot be consoled; sufferings that cannot be alleviated. I only wish to—to—

LOUISE *(rising and joining them).* You wish to die.

JEAN *(rises).* Who told you so? How do you know I want to die?

LOUISE. I feel it while I listen to you. Do you not know that we who are blind can listen with our whole being?

HENRIETTE. Tell us your troubles.

JEAN. I cannot—I am pursued by officers of the law. I have no strength to fly further; they will arrest me.

HENRIETTE. What have you done?

JEAN. I have stolen.

*(*HENRIETTE *and* LOUISE *recoil a moment.)*

Stolen money confided to my care. All the meager savings of a poor workman. I did not steal it for myself, but for *him*, for a wretch whom I despise, but whom, alas, I love!

(Loud voices heard in cafe—laughter.)

JACQUES *(in the cafe).* Come—order anything you want—I'll stand it.

JEAN *(crosses to L.).* Listen—that is his voice. He is there, wasting in debauchery the money purchased by my crime. When I am away from him, reason returns, and I hate his baseness. Alas! But when he speaks to me—touches me—my hate disappears. I tremble at his touch and am his slave. I steal for him—I almost believe I would kill at his bidding! You see, it is better that I should die! *(goes R.)*

HENRIETTE *(stopping her).* You cannot atone for a fault by taking your life.

JEAN. If I am found, they will arrest—imprison me.

LOUISE. When you have left the prison, you will have paid the debt you owe to man.

HENRIETTE. And repentance will pay the debt you owe to Heaven.

JEAN. I cannot believe that there is a Heaven for an outcast like me.

LOUISE. Oh, unhappy woman!

HENRIETTE *(pointing to the river).* See where such a belief would lead you. Listen and believe us. You can redeem your past and your future will be happier. *(Slips money into her hand.)* Take this!

JEAN *(refusing).* No, no!

LOUISE. Do not refuse, I implore you.

JEAN *(weeping).* Ah, you are right. There must indeed be a Heaven, for has it not sent two angels to succor and save me? *(She takes their hands and weeps over them.)*

HENRIETTE. Courage, courage!

JEAN. Yes, yes, I will have courage. I'll fly from Paris—from him. Have I the strength? I do not know! I only know I wish I could give my life for you.

(JACQUES appears at door of cafe.)

May Heaven bless you. Farewell! *(Crosses to R., goes to exit.)*

JACQUES *(calling after her).* Jeanette?

(JEANETTE stops suddenly; does not turn.)

LOUISE *(to HENRIETTE).* What is she doing?

HENRIETTE. Alas! She stops!

JACQUES. Where are you going?

JEAN *(with averted head).* Away from you—away—and I hope never to see you again.

JACQUES *(coming out and going to her).* Bah! You don't want to see me? *(Takes her hand.)* Then why did you stop when I called? What makes your hand tremble?

JEAN. It does not tremble. I have found strength to resist you. I am ashamed of the life I lead, and of the infamy into which you have plunged me.

JACQUES. Pooh! Pooh! Put all that stuff out of your head and follow me.

JEAN *(disengaging hand).* I will not!

JACQUES. You must—enough of this foolishness. Come! Do you hear?

JEAN *(hesitates).* I—I—*(Looks at girls and gains courage.)* Yes, I hear and I refuse. I will not obey you.

JACQUES. Do you want me to persuade you in the usual way?

JEAN. You shall not. Never again.

JACQUES *(threateningly).* We'll see! *(Rushes upon her.)*

(At the same moment a policeman enters L. JEANETTE, *looking around for some means of escape, sees him.)*

JEAN. Ah, you *shall* see! *(To* OFFICER.*)* Monsieur, arrest me! I am a thief!

OFFICER. Arrest you? Who are you?

JEAN. My name is Jeanette Girard. Officers are in search of me. I escaped from them an hour ago. Now I wish to deliver myself to justice.

JACQUES *(goes up to hide himself).* She has gone crazy.

*(*OFFICER *takes paper from his belt and looks at it.)*

OFFICER. Jeanette Girard. Yes, accused of theft.

JEAN *(looking at* JACQUES*).* Of which I am guilty.

OFFICER. Well, if you confess it, I must take you to prison.

JEAN *(to* OFFICER*).* Come! *(She takes his arm. As they pass* JACQUES, *she stops.)* My expiation begins. Pray Heaven that I may complete it. I said I would escape this time. You see—I keep my word!

(Exit JEANETTE *and* OFFICER.*)*

JACQUES. She is a fool! Humph! *(He exits into cafe.)*

(Singing and noise continue.)

LOUISE. Henriette.

HENRIETTE. You are frightened, sister.

LOUISE. Yes, yes, I am, indeed.

HENRIETTE. And night is falling fast.

LOUISE. Why doesn't Monsieur Martin come?

(Enter ANTOINE.*)*

ANTOINE. Here I am, Mademoiselle.

HENRIETTE *(with joy).* Ah!

LOUISE. At last!

HENRIETTE. We began to be very anxious!

ANTOINE. You must excuse me, for I live a great distance from here.

HENRIETTE *(astonished).* A great distance?

LOUISE. Why, we were told your house was but a few steps from the bridge.

ANTOINE *(aside).* A mistake. *(Aloud.)* Yes, yes, indeed it was—that is, I did live but a short distance from here, but you see, I have moved. Come, come, let us go, mademoiselle!

HENRIETTE *(shrinking from him, in doubt).* You have moved?

ANTOINE. Yes, yes, only yesterday.

LOUISE. And you said nothing of it in your letter.

ANTOINE. No, I did not write it because—because—in short, I didn't know I was going to move. But if you doubt me, here's a neighbor of mine—a good, honest citizen—he will vouch for me.

*(*ANTOINE *makes a sign and* PICARD *enters.)*

HENRIETTE *(crossing and looking at him).* Honest citizen?

LOUISE *(extending her hands).* Henriette, do not leave me.

(The men seize HENRIETTE, *place a handkerchief over her mouth and carry her off.)*

HENRIETTE *(as she is carried off)*. No! No! Help, help!

LOUISE *(alone)*. I hear nothing. Henriette, where is that man? Sister, why do you not answer me? *(With terror.)* Henriette, Henriette! Speak to me. Speak one word. Answer me. Henriette! *(With despair.)* No answer!

HENRIETTE *(heard in distance with stifled voice)*. Louise!

LOUISE *(screaming)*. Henriette, Henriette! Ah! 'Tis she! They have dragged her away from me! Oh, what shall I do? Alone! Alone! Abandoned! What will become of me? Alone in this great city, helpless and blind? *(She breaks down weeping, after a pause. She gropes her way up the stage and reaches the stone coping of the quay over the river. Just as she does so, she stumbles as though about to fall into the river.)*

(PIERRE, entering at R., catches her in his arms just in time to save her.)

PIERRE *(brings her down C.)*. Great Heavens! What were you going to do?

LOUISE *(trembling with fright)*. Nothing, nothing. What was it?

PIERRE. Another step and you would have fallen into the river.

LOUISE. Oh, save me, save me!

(Enter LA FROCHARD from cafe.)

FRO. Why, what is the matter? What are you doing there, Pierre?

LOUISE. Ah, madame, do not leave me! I beg you, I entreat you, do not leave me here all alone.

FRO. What is it? Have you lost your head?

LOUISE. Alas! Madame, a few minutes ago my sister was here with me, and they have stolen her away from me.

PIERRE. Stolen her?

FRO. Well, you must let your parents know.

LOUISE. Our parents? Alas, madame, we are orphans!

PIERRE. You have acquaintances—friends—

LOUISE. We have only just arrived in Paris and I know no one here.

FRO. No one? No one at all?

PIERRE. Were the people who took your sister away gentlemen or common people?

LOUISE. How can I tell?

FRO. You could see their clothes.

LOUISE. Alas! Madame, I am blind!

PIERRE. You are blind?

FRO. Blind, without relations, friends or acquaintances in Paris. *(Looks at her.)* And young and pretty.

PIERRE *(aside and low)*. It is true, young and pretty.

FRO *(to PIERRE)*. Go! Leave me alone with her; I'll take care of her.

PIERRE. Yes, mother. We must help her to find her sister.

FRO. That's all right. I know what to do. You clear out.

(PIERRE crosses to wheel.)

LOUISE *(uneasily)*. You will not leave me, madame?

FRO. Never fear, my dear, I'll not leave you.

PIERRE *(goes up and takes his wheel).* Blind! So young and pretty. *(Laughing sadly to himself.)* Pretty! What is that to you, wretched one? *(Exit L.)*

FRO. Come, come, my pretty child, don't be downcast.

LOUISE. Alas! To whom shall I go for help?

FRO. To me. I am an honest woman, mother of a family. I'll give you a home until you find your sister.

LOUISE. Ah! Madame, you are very good to have pity on me. But we will find her, won't we?

FRO. Oh yes, certainly, in time. *(Aside.)* And we'll take plenty of time! *(To* LOUISE.*)* Come, then come along with me.

LOUISE. I trust myself to you, madame.

FRO. You couldn't do better. You have fallen into good hands. Come!

CURTAIN

SCENE TWO

SCENE: *The beautifully furnished apartment of* BARON DE VAUDREY, *with satin drapes and elegant decorations. The lights are low. It is early evening. As the curtain rises,* ANTOINE *and* PICARD *carry* HENRIETTE *into apartment and place her on couch. They are arguing.*

PICARD. I tell you, my master may return at any moment.

ANTOINE. And what of it? She'll come around and we'll be on our way in no time.

PICARD. How is she? Is she coming to?

ANTOINE. No, curse her! She's still as death! Think of something, Picard—how do you revive such a one? Oh, I've never had such troubles with any of them before!

PICARD. What if my former master, Count Levant, the new Minister of Police, finds out about this? He'll put me in the Bastille for sure! Since he's taken this new post, he's hard as stone and cold as a fish. Why, he even plans to put a stop to everyone's amusements, and if he knew about the Marquis de Menton's place and these abductions— oh, oh, look at her, she's going to die on us!

ANTOINE *(fans her frantically, rubs her wrists).* No, no! Oh, how did I know she'd be ill and faint? I thought these peasant girls were supposed to be strong and sturdy. You know, we couldn't keep her in the streets in this state.

PICARD. I know—I know, but why did we bring her here? Oh heaven, this is the end of me! My master will discharge me, Count Levant will chastise me, and there isn't a gentleman in Paris will engage me once it's known I've been caught in such an affair! Ah, I remember, the master has some smelling salts! I'll get them.

(He goes off and returns with vial, hands it to ANTOINE. *Both bend over her. Enter* BARON MAURICE DE VAUDREY, *a young nobleman. He has an air of wealth and privilege.)*

DE VAUDREY. Picard!

PICARD. Wait a moment, master! Let me explain—the young lady has fainted!

DE VAUDREY. So I see!

PICARD. And my friend here is trying to revive her.

ANTOINE *(interrupting)*. Your valet has accommodated me, sir. I was on my way to take this young lady to the residence of your friend, the Marquis de Menton. She became ill and faint, and so I brought her here.

DE VAUDREY. Ah—de Menton. Yes, I understand. Well, do what you can for her and get her out of here.

PICARD. But master, what if she wakens here? She will remember the place and will expose you.

DE VAUDREY. Expose me? And who would she be to expose me? I am tired of the pretense of these willingly abducted maidens! When the proper moment arrives, she will awake and go through it all. "Where am I?" "Why have you brought me here?" *(Laughs.)* And then by slow degrees this profound and virtuous despair, which commenced in a torrent of tears, will be drowned in—a flood of champagne!

(DE VAUDREY turns his back during this speech. HENRIETTE *gradually comes to, raises herself.)*

HENRIETTE. Am I mad? Do I dream?

DE VAUDREY. Now, that is singular. Something of an improvement, at least.

HENRIETTE *(rises and speaks to* ANTOINE *in a decisive tone)*. How has this outrage been committed? Is this your house?

ANTOINE. Ah, mademoiselle, you do me honor! It is not for myself—

HENRIETTE. Not another word, sir. I wish to return this very instant to the place where my sister awaits me. Come, take me back at once.

ANTOINE *(firmly)*. Mademoiselle, after all the trouble I have had, you can scarcely suppose we will let you go. No, I shall take you to the Chateau du Bel Air.

(He grabs her arm. She gasps, jerks free from him.)

HENRIETTE. Listen, sir! I see the horrible trap you have laid for me. But you, vile as you are, can scarcely understand the extent of your own villainy. You have separated me from a poor child whose only help in life I am, whose misfortunes command the respect of criminals even worse than yourself. She is dependent on me alone. Without me she cannot take a single step, for she is blind!

ALL. Blind?

HENRIETTE. Yes, blind, and alone! Alone in Paris, without money, without help, wandering through the streets, sightless, homeless, wild with despair. What will become of her? She is blind! Do you hear me? She is blind!

ANTOINE *(trying to placate her, keeping his eye on* DE VAUDREY*).* Compose yourself, mademoiselle. I will have a search made for her tomorrow. I will find her and bring her to you.

HENRIETTE. Bring her—my little sister Louise to the Chateau du Bel Air—to a house of sin! No—no—never! Is this the only answer you have to my prayer? Are there no more gentlemen then of honor in Paris?

*(*DE VAUDREY *turns suddenly in anger, crosses to her.)*

DE VAUDREY. Take my hand, mademoiselle. I will conduct you to safety.

HENRIETTE. Oh, thank you, monsieur!

ANTOINE *(quickly bars the way).* Excuse me, sir, but you cannot do this. I have promised the Marquis and if I am further delayed—

DE VAUDREY *(coldly).* Miserable scoundrel—give me room!

ANTOINE *(pulls pistol).* Even though you are the Baron De Vaudrey, you do not take my bread!

DE VAUDREY *(knocks pistol from his hand, trips him and knocks him to the floor).* Picard! If you are my man and not the tool of this filth, tie him and hold him here!

*(*PICARD *comes and begins to tie* ANTOINE.)*

Come, mademoiselle, later I shall attend to your abductor! And, if I'm not mistaken, the Marquis may also live to regret the day he sent you off on this errand!

CURTAIN

ACT TWO

SCENE ONE

SCENE: *The private office of the Minister of Police.* COUNT EDMUND LE-
VANT *is discovered seated at table R.C. He is in his late fifties. His carriage
and appearance indicate that is is accustomed to authority. He is well
and formally dressed. His table is covered with papers which he is in the
act of signing, hastily reading them over.* CHIEF CLERK *is at the table,
standing in a respectful attitude.*

LEVANT. I regret that my recent accession to the position of Minister of Police compels me to occupy so much of your time.

CLERK. I am entirely at your service, my lord.

LEVANT. I am desirous that a stop should be put to the scandals
which disgraced the preceding administration. *(Taking up paper and
rising.)*, I have here a report which needs explanation. How is it
possible that a young girl could be abducted in the open street at
eight o'clock in the evening, and there should be no one to oppose
such an outrage?

CLERK. There are scoundrels in Paris audacious and dexterous
enough to do anything, sir.

LEVANT. Where were the police?

CLERK. The police have discovered the abductor and compelled
him to confess; however, the chief actor who planned the affair has
never been apprehended.

LEVANT. Three months have elapsed since this most daring outrage,
and the really guilty one, you say, has not been punished?

CLERK *(in a very meaning tone).* That is due, my lord, to certain
circumstances.

LEVANT. What circumstances? To whom does this Chateau du Bel
Air belong?

CLERK. To the Marquis de Menton.

LEVANT. De Menton! An ancient and illustrious family, whose last
scion would nonetheless stake all its glories on the cast of a die—a
worthless rake! But the girl—what became of her?

CLERK. She was carried off—by—by—by—well, a person un-
friendly to the Marquis.

LEVANT. His name—speak, sir.

CLERK *(after a pause).* The Baron Maurice De Vaudrey.

LEVANT *(astonished).* My nephew! H—mm. I appreciate the sentiment that caused you to hesitate, but for the future, sir, remember
that justice is no respecter of persons.

CLERK. Do you wish, my lord, that this affair should be entered in
the secret archives of the police?

LEVANT. The secret archives of the police? Do such records really
exist?

CLERK. Certainly, my lord. The secret and complete history of every noble family in France may be found there. You have but to mention a name and in five minutes the desired volumes will be in your hands.

LEVANT. Very well, then. If the history of the house of De Vaudrey is there, let that history be complete!

CLERK. I shall obey you, my lord! *(He salutes and exits.)*

*(*PICARD *enters.)*

LEVANT *(seated)*. Ah, Picard! I am glad to see you. I wish to speak to you of your master. How is he behaving himself?

PICARD. With all respect, my lord, his conduct is scandalous, perfectly scandalous.

LEVANT. Am I to understand that you wish to leave his service?

PICARD. Yes, my lord! The Baron, your nephew, has principles which I can no longer accept. Although the Baron thinks it proper to compromise his nobility, I cannot compromise my livery.

LEVANT. Very well, I will take you back into my service!

PICARD *(joyfully)*. You will? Ah, my lord, you have relieved me, and I resume my personal dignity.

LEVANT. On one condition. I wish you to remain for a time with my nephew. It is important that I should know his movements. I could employ the police, but I have already learned too much from them, and through you, who are attached to him, I desire to know the rest.

PICARD. The rest? What has he been doing? You frighten me. What do the police know?

LEVANT. They know that after the duel—

PICARD *(starts)*. The duel! What duel?

LEVANT. Do not pretend that you do not know that he dangerously wounded the Marquis de Menton in a duel about a woman!

PICARD *(bewildered, still pretending innocence)*. He fought a duel and dangerously wounded his antagonist, and about a woman? Oh, the sly dog, and I wanted to leave him!

LEVANT. No, no, not yet. I desire that you remain with him and discover where he hides himself.

PICARD. I only know, sir, that he advises me he will not need my services for days on end. He spends his evenings, many of them, quietly at home, and alone, sir. But perhaps there's hope—perhaps there is a woman. I'll discover the saucy little beauty for whom he neglects all of his friends. Of course she must be little and saucy— that's the style I like!

LEVANT. Oh, indeed!

PICARD *(with relish)*. Doubtless he has done everything in good style—has taken some elegant, quiet little house, rooms hung with velvet, all that sort of thing—

LEVANT. Why, at that rate, you will ruin your master.

PICARD *(assuming the airs of a gentleman)*. Bah! If she is worth the trouble, where is the harm in a little ruin?

LEVANT. There, that will do for today!

(The COUNTESS DIANE LEVANT, *wife of* COUNT LEVANT, *and aunt to the* BARON MAURICE DE VAUDREY, *appears at the back. She is a very attractive woman in her mid-forties, well and carefully dressed. Her education and good breeding are apparent.)*
Go, and do not forget my orders.

PICARD. I will obey them, my lord! Baron, you are a sly dog, and I thought you a saint! *(Salutes the Countess as she enters. Exit.)*

COUNTESS. Monsieur, I am informed you wished to speak with me.

LEVANT. I was about to come to you, but you have anticipated me. I desire to speak with you on the subject of your nephew, the Baron De Vaudrey, and to ask you to prepare him for a marriage which His Majesty —

COUNTESS *(sadly)*. Wishes to impose upon him. *(Sits.)*

LEVANT. Impose on him? A magnificent alliance which will complete the measure of the distinguished honors with which his Majesty deigns to favor me.

COUNTESS. What miracle has worked this change in you? You, whose life passed so quietly at our dear home in Dauphine, far from the intrigue of the court. *(Looking him steadily in the face.)* You have become ambitious — and of what?

LEVANT. Yes, I am ambitious.

COUNTESS *(sadly)*. I cannot believe it!

LEVANT. Diane, my wife, I have vainly sought every means in my power to dispel the melancholy which has never left you since the first days of our marriage. Share with me the glorious task I have undertaken. Is it not a noble privilege to have the power to seek out and console those that weep, to assist the suffering, to relieve the misery of the unfortunate? Can you not share my ambition with me to do good?

COUNTESS *(shrinking from him)*. Ah! I did not think of the limitless power placed in your hands, a power before which all doors are opened, a power that can penetrate all secrets — perhaps, enable you to discover —

LEVANT *(astonished)*. Discover? What?

COUNTESS *(recovering herself)*. The extent, as you say, of the misery in this great city.

(Enter DE VAUDREY *at back.)*
Ah, Maurice!

DE VAUDREY. My dear aunt!

LEVANT. Baron! I am glad to see you. The Countess and myself have an important communication to make to you.

DE VAUDREY. I regret that I should have been detained.

LEVANT. My dear Maurice, his Majesty did me the honor to receive me yesterday, and he spoke of you.

DE VAUDREY. Of me?

LEVANT. He takes a great interest in your welfare. He wishes you to accept a position at the court, and desires at the same time that you should marry.

DE VAUDREY. Marry?

COUNTESS. My dear nephew, have no fear that his choice will do violence to your feelings. The lady whom he has chosen has youth, beauty and fortune.

LEVANT. In proof of which I have only to tell you that his choice is Mademoiselle—

DE VAUDREY. Do not name her.

LEVANT. Why not?

DE VAUDREY. I refuse to marry.

LEVANT. Before committing yourself irrevocably, Maurice, reflect. This marriage is an honor which his Majesty desires to confer upon you, and when he speaks—

DE VAUDREY. I will go to him. I will thank him for his goodness, I will place my services at his disposal; my devotion, my life, if need be, are his, but my affections are my own, and I wish to remain— free.

LEVANT. Free! Free to lead a life of dissipation which you may not always be able to hide from the world.

DE VAUDREY. There is nothing in my life to hide.

LEVANT *(severely)*. Are you sure of that, Baron?

DE VAUDREY. Monsieur!

COUNTESS *(rising anxiously and interfering)*. Maurice! *(To* LEVANT.*)* My husband! Defer this for the present —permit me—

LEVANT. Very well, we will return to this another time. *(*DE VAUDREY *attempts to answer him.* COUNTESS *makes a mute appeal to him and he refrains.)* I leave you with the Countess, and I hope that your respect and affection for her will lend more weight to her counsel than you are disposed to give to mine. *(Exit.)*

COUNTESS *(crossing to* DE VAUDREY*)*. Who is this woman you love? What obstacle prevents the avowal of your affection?

DE VAUDREY. Ah! Where shall I find a heart like yours? You have divined my secret. I love a young girl, as charming as she is pure. I love her, yet my lips have never sought hers. I adore her, yet I have never dared to whisper my passion.

COUNTESS. Her name? Her family?

DE VAUDREY. She is born of the people. She is an orphan and lives by the labor of her hands.

COUNTESS. And you would make such a one your wife?

DE VAUDREY. Do not judge her until you have seen her. Consent to see her; then advise me.

COUNTESS. In such a marriage there can be no happiness for you, and for her only misery.

DE VAUDREY *(with force)*. Can *you* tell me that? You who have been the victim of a blind obedience which has sacrificed your life?

COUNTESS *(uttering a cry)*. How do you know? Who has torn aside the veil from my secret?

DE VAUDREY *(taking her hand)*. There was but one soul in all this world tender and noble enough to appreciate and sustain your own in its trials. Your dearly beloved sister! My mother! In her last moments she exacted from me the promise to devote myself to you, should misfortune ever come, and I gladly gave my word.

COUNTESS. Ah, yes. I was young and mad—I loved and was loved without knowing wrong. I consented to a secret marriage with a man beneath me in rank. They thought him my lover and killed him almost under my very eyes—and I was a mother. Family honor demanded that my child should disappear, because my hand was promised to the Count Levant. I consoled myself with the hope that perhaps I should see her again some day. Alas! The days have passed into months, the months into years, and all my prayers are in vain.

DE VAUDREY. My poor aunt. They were indeed cruel.

COUNTESS. So cruel that often I ask myself if it would not have been better had they killed me, too. And my child. May she not cry out from the depths of her despair, "Accursed be my unnatural mother!" I hear that cry always—it pursues me in my prayers, torments my dreams—I hear it always, always!

(LEVANT *enters at back and stands unobserved.*)

DE VAUDREY. Then do you, who have suffered so much, who suffer still, counsel me to obey? Would you have me chain my life to one woman, while my heart is filled with the image of another? Will you advise me to do this?

COUNTESS (*very emphatically*). No, no, never! (*Turns and sees* LEVANT, *speaks to him.*) Ah, Monsieur, have pity on him, do not ask him to stifle the cry of his conscience.

DE VAUDREY (*unobserved by* LEVANT *and in a low voice*). Take care!

(*The* COUNTESS *checks herself and stands in dejected attitude before her husband.*)

LEVANT (*severely*). Madame! To whom do you refer? Of what are you speaking?

COUNTESS (*trembling*). I meant—I spoke of—

DE VAUDREY. Monsieur, the words of the Countess are but the echo of those she just heard me utter. They are but the irrevocable revolt of my heart against the marriage and the suffering you would impose upon me.

LEVANT (*coldly*). Madame, had your words no other meaning?

COUNTESS. No, no. I am agitated, Monsieur; I am ill.

LEVANT. That is evident. Maurice, conduct the Countess to her carriage.

(DE VAUDREY *bows to* LEVANT, *offers his hand to the Countess and both exit, followed by the gaze of* LEVANT. *When they reach the exit,* LEVANT *speaks.*)

And return immediately. I desire to speak with you.

(*Exit* COUNTESS *and* DE VAUDREY. LEVANT *goes to his desk, writes on a paper, and rings a bell.* CHIEF CLERK *appears.*)

LEVANT. Take this to the keeper of the secret records, and return with what he gives you.

(DE VAUDREY *re-enters.* CLERK *salutes and exits.*)

LEVANT. Baron, you can readily understand that propriety and considerations for my own dignity induced me to accept the explanation made by you on behalf of the Countess.

DE VAUDREY. Monsieur!

LEVANT. You also understand that that explanation did not satisfy me.

DE VAUDREY. Well, sir, what are you pleased to think?

LEVANT. I think, sir, that the Countess wept not for you, but for herself. You spoke of her early life, which is shrouded in some dark secret, and which is the torment of her life and mine. Speak, Baron, what is it?

DE VAUDREY. Monsieur Levant?

LEVANT. I command you to speak.

DE VAUDREY. I know nothing, sir.

LEVANT. Very well—you choose to forget all you owe to me. Twice today you have refused obedience—nevertheless, I will know the secret which you refuse to disclose.

DE VAUDREY. I am ignorant of the secret to which you refer.

(CLERK *returns with a large folio in his hand, which he gives to* LEVANT, *salutes and exits.*)

LEVANT. Then we will learn it together.

DE VAUDREY. What are you going to do?

LEVANT. Here—here in the archives of the Police are entered the secrets of every noble family in France. Here I will learn the secret of Diane De Vaudrey, Countess Levant!

DE VAUDREY (*while* LEVANT *is turning over leaves*). Why, that would be shameful! Infamous!

LEVANT. Hmmm—yes, here it is. House of De Vaudrey, and each member has a page. Ah, Diane Eleanor, daughter of the Count Francois De Vaudrey.

DE VAUDREY (*crosses rapidly towards the table and places his open hand on the pages*). Monsieur, that you must not read!

LEVANT (*starting up*). What do you mean?

DE VAUDREY. I mean that the act you are about to commit is unworthy of you—you must not, you shall not!

LEVANT. Who will prevent it?

DE VAUDREY. Your own honor, which will revolt against such treason. Ah, sir, if your own honor does not speak loud enough, I will!

LEVANT. You?

(DE VAUDREY *crumples up the page under his hand, tears it from the book and puts it in his bosom. Puts his hand to his pistol.*)

DE VAUDREY. I warn you, sir, that you can only wrest this paper from me with my life. You shall kill me before I part with it. Remember, sir, that it is not alone her secret I have saved you from violating; 'tis your own dignity and self-respect. I defend your honor against yourself. (LEVANT *bows his head.*)

CURTAIN

SCENE TWO

SCENE: *The open square in front of the Church of St. Sulpice, including church portico and steps. The ground is lightly covered with snow.* PIERRE *is discovered seated on a stool.*

PIERRE. Nearly twelve o'clock; they will soon be here.

(JACQUES *enters at back.*)

JACQUES *(to* PIERRE*)*. The women have not come yet?

PIERRE. No, not yet.

JACQUES. They ought to be here. The service will soon be over and they will miss the charitable idiots.

PIERRE. Ah, you need not worry about them. Jacques, I have a favor to ask of you.

JACQUES. If it is money, I haven't got any!

PIERRE. No—it is not money. Look, Jacques, when you are angry with me, curse me, beat me, if you want to, but do not call me "cripple"—not—not when Louise is present.

JACQUES *(surprised).* Ah—ah, indeed! We must speak to Monsieur respectfully—take off our hats, I suppose.

PIERRE *(supplicatingly).* Jacques!

JACQUES. So it hurts your feelings to be called cripple, does it? Well, look at yourself.

PIERRE. I know I am ugly—almost deformed—and yet, who, when I was an infant, beat me and twisted my limbs?

JACQUES. That is enough. As you don't want to be called "cripple" any more—I'll rechristen you "Cupid."

PIERRE *(discouraged).* Do as you like.

JACQUES. Now I come to think of it, it is only when Louise is about that you object to being called cripple. Perhaps you are in love with her.

PIERRE. What do you mean?

JACQUES. You are not so stupid, after all. She is blind and does not know the difference between a handsome man like me and a miserable abortion like you. Oh, ha! You're in love, in love with a blind girl. Ha, ha, ha!

PIERRE. I? I? In love?

JACQUES. Why then are you ashamed of being called cripple before her? Afraid she'll find you out?

PIERRE. I want to think there is one in the world who does not regard me with disgust. But—in love with her—she who is beautiful enough, good enough, to be an angel!

JACQUES. I don't know or care anything about her goodness. I know that her eyes are more use to her now than if she could see with them. *(Goes up.)*

PIERRE *(to himself.)* Yes, yes, she is blind, but her face is so sweet that it would move a stone to pity. And her great beautiful eyes seem to look at me so truthfully that I almost fear she can see me.

JACQUES *(coming down L.)*. Come along, I want you, Cupid.

PIERRE *(rousing himself)*. No, I won't.

JACQUES. Rebellion, eh! Now do as I order you or look out for a beating.

PIERRE. Jacques, you're straight and strong and I must submit to you, but when I see the use you make of your strength, I am satisfied with my miserable weakness.

(JACQUES shrugs his shoulders. At the same time LOUISE is heard singing outside.)

JACQUES. Ah, here they are at last.

(LOUISE's song continues approaching.)

That voice ought to be worth a louis a day at least.

(Enter LOUISE led by LA FROCHARD. LOUISE is miserably dressed in rags and bits of clothing. She is pale and wan, and walks with faltering steps, continuing her song. LA FROCHARD goes around to people near stage.)

FRO. Pity a poor, unhappy, blind child. Charity, if you please. Ah! there's nothing to be got from these miserable common people. They will stop and listen to the singing quick enough, but when you ask them for a sou they clear out. *(Takes LOUISE by the arm.)* Come, come, let's be moving.

LOUISE. I am very tired, Madame. We have walked so much today.

FRO. Well, didn't you want to walk? Didn't you say you wanted to look for your sister?

LOUISE. Yes, but you always walk in the same part of the city.

FRO. Bah! How do you know? You can't see.

LOUISE. I know that, madame, but when you found me you promised—

FRO. I promised to help you look for your sister. Still, you have to earn your bread. You sing and I'll do the begging.

LOUISE *(weeping)*. I'll sing, madame, if you wish it.

JACQUES. Yes, but how do you sing? Like a mourner at a funeral.

LOUISE *(weeping)*. I sing as well as I can. But when I think of what I am—of what I am doing—I—I—*(Breaks down entirely, sobs.)* I am so unahppy—so miserably unhappy.

PIERRE *(starts forward)*. Louise!

JACQUES *(pushing him)*. Hello, what are you up to, Master Cupid?

PIERRE. Nothing, nothing. *(Aside.)* I am so helpless.

JACQUES *(looking at LOUISE)*. She is pretty when she cries.

FRO *(to LOUISE)*. Come, come. Enough of that. Let us be moving.

LOUISE *(tries to wipe her eyes)*. Very well, madame. I will.

FRO *(stops her)*. Don't do that. What! Wipe away real tears? Why, that is just the thing to catch the soft-hearted fools.

(A man crosses, sees LOUISE, stops a moment, slips a coin in her hand, and exits into church. LA FROCHARD takes the money.)

Go on singing. Have pity on a poor blind child. Charity, good people, if you please.

(LA FROCHARD *and* LOUISE *exit R.,* JACQUES *and* PIERRE *L. Organ music begins.* DOCTOR *enters from the church. Middle-aged and very dignified, he is the doctor of the hospital and prison. He is professionally garbed, carries a doctor's bag. His manner is warm and concerned. Enter* COUNTESS *from L.)*

COUNTESS. Ah, Doctor, I am glad to see you.

DOCTOR. Because it is not a professional visit, I suppose?

COUNTESS. No, I am always happy to receive you as a friend.

DOCTOR. And not as a physician. I understand, Countess. Will you then permit me, as a friend, to advise you?

COUNTESS. Doctor, I assure you I am not ill. You are mistaken.

DOCTOR. Very well then, Madame, I will concede that you are in perfect health. Pardon me for speaking thus plainly to you, but I have already been consulted by —

COUNTESS *(startled).* My husband?

DOCTOR. The Count Levant has imparted to me the great anxiety he feels for you.

COUNTESS. What did he say?

DOCTOR. That you are wearing yourself out with a secret grief.

COUNTESS. Alas! Yes. What am I to do?

DOCTOR. Address yourself to the Great Physician. *(Pointing to church.)* There you will learn that the heaviest burden is easier borne when shared by one who has the right to know your inmost thoughts.

COUNTESS. You mean my husband. Impossible!

DOCTOR. No, no! Not impossible. A generous heart like his will appreciate your confidence. Seek strength here, madame! *(Leads her to church.)*

COUNTESS. I thank you, doctor. Ah! If one such friend as you had been given me years ago, I might have been spared this anguish. *(Exit into church.)*

DOCTOR. Ah! What a strange thing is human nature.

(Goes up C. As he starts to go, LA FROCHARD *and* LOUISE *appear R.)*

FRO. Pity for a poor blind child, if you please, charity.

DOCTOR. Blind? Who? This young girl? *(Coming forward.)*

FRO. Alas! Yes, my good sir, pity.

DOCTOR. Poor unhappy child, at your age. Let me look at your eyes.

FRO *(harshly interposing).* What for?

DOCTOR. Come here, my child. Let me see your eyes. I am a doctor!

LOUISE *(joyfully).* A doctor?

FRO *(to* LOUISE*).* Come along. *(To* DOCTOR.*)* They can't be cured; it is no use.

DOCTOR. But I insist.

FRO. Well, then, see for yourself if she is not blind. *(Passing* LOUISE *across. Aside.)* Curse him, I know him; he is that whining doctor at the hospital.

LOUISE *(as* DOCTOR *comes to her).* Oh, sir, if you are a doctor —

DOCTOR *(after examining her eyes).* You have not always been blind, my child, have you?

LOUISE. No, monsieur. I was fourteen years old when this misfortune befell me.

DOCTOR. Fourteen? And you have had no treatment?

LOUISE *(quickly)*. Monsieur—

FRO *(interrupting)*. We are so poor, good doctor, we have not the money to—

LOUISE. Oh, monsieur, is there any hope for me?

DOCTOR. Calm yourself, my child, calm yourself. *(He takes* LA FROCHARD *aside L.)* Come here!

FRO *(pushing* LOUISE *back and crossing to* DOCTOR*)*. What is it, doctor?

DOCTOR. Listen, you must not excite her; you must not tell her too suddenly what I hope. Bring her to me at the hospital St. Louis.

FRO. Yes, yes, I know, I have been there often.

DOCTOR. I thought I recognized you. Let me see, you are called Mother—

FRO *(indignantly)*. Widow Frochard, monsieur.

DOCTOR. Yes, I remember. Well, when she is calmer, tell her gently that I think there is hope for her.

FRO. Yes, yes, I will. I'll tell her gently.

DOCTOR *(crosses to* LOUISE*)*. Here, my poor child. *(Giving her a piece of money.)* Courage, my dear, I will see you again. *(Exit R.)*

FRO *(following him to exit)*. May Heaven bless you, good doctor. Heaven bless you. *(After his exit.)* Curses on you for an intermeddling old fool! *(Returns to* LOUISE.*)*

LOUISE. What did he tell you, madame?

FRO. He said it was not worth the trouble. There is no hope for you.

LOUISE. No hope! No hope! Alas! What am I to do?

FRO *(aside)*. If I bring her here every day he will see her again. *(Aloud to* LOUISE.*)* Look you, child, I am a good woman. You have been complaining that I always take you to the same places; now tomorrow we will look for your sister in some other part of the city.

LOUISE. Oh, madame, I thank you. I have now but one hope left, to find my dear sister, my dear Henriette.

*(*PIERRE *enters.)*

FRO *(to* LOUISE*)*. Look you, they will be coming out of the church soon; now sing loud. No laziness, mind you; I'll be watching you. *(Exit* LA FROCHARD.*)*

LOUISE. Yes, madame. *(She sings.)*

LOUISE. (SONG: *"If I Had a Wish"**)

> If I had a wish I'd wish to find,
> Carved upon a tree with hearts entwined,
> Names of all the beaus that the future holds
> So that we could guess our betrothed.

*Music on page 157.

Everyone wants to meet a wise man
Like the books reveal.
He would say magic words and then—

(She breaks down in sobs.)

LOUISE *(sits on steps and tries to cover herself with her rags).* I am so cold.
*(*PIERRE *takes off his coat, snow begins to fall.)*
I am so very cold.
*(*PIERRE *puts his coat on her shoulders.)*
Ah, is that you, Pierre?
PIERRE. Yes, mamselle.
LOUISE. Yes, it must be you, Pierre. You are the only one who is kind to me. *(Touches his coat.)* But this is your coat! What will you do without it, Pierre?
PIERRE. Oh! I'll do very well, indeed mamselle. I have my jacket, and my woolen waistcoat, and my—oh, that is only my overcoat. *(He shivers.)*
LOUISE. Pierre, without you I should die.
PIERRE *(seating himself beside her).* I know they make you wretched, but I am helpless. I can do nothing.
LOUISE. Is your sympathy, your compassion, nothing? *(She touches coat on her shoulders. She gives her hand to him, which he grasps eagerly. She touches his shoulder with the other hand and discovers that he is in shirt sleeves.)* Oh, how selfish I am! *(She takes off coat and offers it to him.)*
PIERRE. No, no!
LOUISE. Pierre, do, do, my dear Pierre, for my sake. *(He takes coat, kisses her hand, and puts arm around her shoulders.)* I am not cold now. Did they not leave me in the cold garret to starve because I refused to beg?
PIERRE *(looking around).* Have you never thought of escaping? I can help you. Let me inform the police and they will protect you.
LOUISE. No, no, you must not. I have thought of it, but that would deprive me of the only chance of finding my sister. They would shut me up in an asylum for the blind. Besides, I have an idea which sustains me. If they take me from one quarter to another, perhaps some day my voice may reach my sister's ears. I will sing the songs we learned together and when I finish I will cry out, "Henriette, 'tis I, your sister Louise. Do you hear me, Henriette, sister?"
(Organ heard playing softly.)
PIERRE. Hush. Mother may hear you! She will be coming back any minute to watch you. *(Rises and helps her up.)*
LOUISE *(rising).* You are right. If she does not hear me singing, she will beat me.
PIERRE. I'll not be far away. *(Exit L.)*

(LOUISE *sings same ballad as before. The* COUNTESS *comes out of the church and stands on the steps.)*

COUNTESS. I have prayed to Heaven to restore to me my child. Will my prayer be answered?

*(*LOUISE *sings.* COUNTESS *starts off and is arrested by the sound of* LOUISE's *voice.)*

What a voice! How tender, how sad! *(Approaches* LOUISE.*)* My child, can you not see me?

(Enter LA FROCHARD *quickly. She stops and looks on.)*

LOUISE. No, madame!

COUNTESS. Poor child! You have relations—a mother?

LOUISE. Mother!

FRO *(seizes* LOUISE *by the wrist).* Yes, my beautiful lady. She has a good mother, if I do say so.

COUNTESS. Is this your daughter?

FRO. The youngest of seven that Heaven has blessed me with, my lady. *(Tightens her grip threateningly on* LOUISE, *who bows her head.)* Isn't that so, my dear?

COUNTESS. She seems to be ill and suffering.

FRO. Ah! Good charitable souls, like you, my lady, have pity on her. She has a nice, good home. Haven't you, my darling? *(Aside, threatens.)* Speak out! *(Twists her arm.)*

LOUISE *(with great effort).* Yes, yes.

COUNTESS *(gives her money).* Give this to your mother and pray for me. *(Exit.)*

LOUISE. I will, madame.

FRO *(seizes* LOUISE's *hand and snatches the money.)* Ah! A louis, another gold piece! A good day, after all. Come on and sing out, sing.

(She heads LOUISE *upstage.* LOUISE *sings as she walks off R.* PIERRE *enters L. and starts across, is about to follow them when* JACQUES, *entering from L., follows him and strikes him heavily on shoulder.* PIERRE *turns.)*

JACQUES. Stop. I have a word to say to you.

PIERRE. What is it?

JACQUES. I forbid you to follow Louise.

PIERRE. What? You forbid?

JACQUES. Yes, and I forbid you to even think of her.

PIERRE. Jacques, I cannot help it. You would not be so cruel. No, no, Jacques. Why are you so cruel?

JACQUES. Never mind why, I forbid you, that is enough, and if you disobey me, I'll twist your miserable legs again, Cupid!

(As JACQUES *speaks, he places both hands on* PIERRE's *and forces him to the ground on his knees.)*

PIERRE. Ah, kill me, kill me, if you will, Jacques. *(Aside.)* But I love her and you cannot forbid that!

CURTAIN

SCENE THREE

SCENE: HENRIETTE's *room, a plainly furnished chamber.* HENRIETTE *is discovered seated at table, sewing.*

HENRIETTE. Three long months since the dreadtul day that robbed me of my darling sister. The Baron De Vaudrey promised he would come today and tell me if he had learned anything. Ah! How I try to cheat myself into the belief that he may bring me news of Louise. I cannot doubt that he loves me, and I madly indulge in dreams of happiness, while my poor Louise is wandering helpless in the streets of this great, heartless city.
(A knock is heard at the door.)
Come in! *(She runs hastily and opens the door.)*
(Enter BARON DE VAUDREY.*)*
DE VAUDREY. Henriette! *(He takes her hand, looks at her steadily a moment. They come downstage. She is agitated.)* Have you heard anything? You seem agitated.
HENRIETTE. I was expecting you. *(Recovering herself.)* I mean I thought, perhaps you would bring me news of Louise.
DE VAUDREY. No, I have heard nothing. Yet you know I have occupied myself unceasingly for the past three months in vain endeavors to ascertain her fate. But, today, Henriette, I wished to speak to you of something else—of myself.
HENRIETTE. I know, monsieur, all that you would say to me. I know that you rescued me from frightful peril, that you fought to defend me, and believe me, I am not ungrateful.
DE VAUDREY. Henriette, do you feel no other sentiment than gratitude? Do you not understand my heart? Until yesterday I was bound in honor to impose silence on my lips. Circumstances have released me, and today I can dare avow with pride—I love you.
HENRIETTE *(grasping the back of chair to support herself).* Oh! This is wrong—wrong. I have known all that your heart was striving to hide from me, and I have been guilty in allowing it to distract me from the only duty I have in life. You should not compel me to confess my weakness.
DE VAUDREY. Henriette!
HENRIETTE. When Louise is restored to my arms, I shall have earned the right to be happy. Then tell me you love me, and I will listen.
DE VAUDREY. Henriette! Henriette! Dear Henriette!
(She gives him her hand; he kisses it warmly. The door opens suddenly and PICARD *appears.)*
PICARD. Don't disturb yourselves.
HENRIETTE *(with a cry).* Ah!
DE VAUDREY. Picard?

PICARD. Yes, monsieur. Picard—only Picard.

DE VAUDREY. What do you want? What brings you here? *(Crosses to* HENRIETTE, *who is at table folding her work.)* Do not be frightened, Henriette. Picard was most ashamed of the affair, and I'll warrant will never get mixed up in another like it, eh?

PICARD *(to* HENRIETTE*).* Believe me, mademoiselle—I never knew— that is, it never occurred to me—

HENRIETTE. Never mind. *(To* DE VAUDREY.*)* I must take my work downstairs, they are waiting for it. *(She goes toward door.)*

DE VAUDREY *(following her).* You will return?

HENRIETTE. Yes, in a few minutes. *(Exit.)*

PICARD *(To* DE VAUDREY*).* So—this is the young man who is studying philosophy!

DE VAUDREY. Well, we are alone now. What brings you here?

PICARD. I took the liberty of following you, monsieur . . .

DE VAUDREY. Following me, you scoundrel!

PICARD *(delighted and aside).* Scoundrel is good—very good. Now he is something like a master.

DE VAUDREY. What do you say?

PICARD. I was saying, monsieur, that scoundrel is not half strong enough, particularly when I come to find out that, after all—

DE VAUDREY. After all? What?

PICARD *(aside).* Good, go on. He will kick me in a minute. *(Aloud.)* You must know, monsieur, that I had become so disgusted with your good conduct that I begged your uncle to relieve me of the duty of serving you any longer, and if he had not insisted on my remaining and watching you—

DE VAUDREY. So, you have become a spy, Master Picard, have you?

PICARD. Yes, sir, a spy on you. *(Aside.)* Now he will kick me. *(Turns and waits.)* No? *(Aloud.)* Why, monsieur, if I had not, how should I have found out that the reason you rescued the little beauty was not to save her—but to save her for your own! You're a gallant—a roué—after all!

DE VAUDREY. Gallant! Roué! *(Laughs.)* Well, how did you find that out?

PICARD. By obeying the instructions of your uncle. I follow you to the house of your inamorata, expecting to find you in the arms of some dark enchantress, and I discover you with this simple country lass.

DE VAUDREY. Believe me, you are quite mistaken in all you have surmised.

PICARD. Oh, you have the fairest of excuses. She is as pretty as—

DE VAUDREY *(interrupting quickly).* Look you, Master Picard, another word and I'll throw you out of the window.

PICARD *(crossing to window and looking out).* Oh, that is going further than I had bargained for. Thrown out of a six-story window.

DE VAUDREY. Listen to me, sir.

PICARD. I am all ears, monsieur, but please to remember that we are very high up.

DE VAUDREY. Return at once to the Count Levant, and tell him that, after having dogged my footsteps day by day, you have found me at last in the presence of the woman I love, and you may inform the count that she is to be my wife.

PICARD *(astounded)*. Your wife? Impossible!

DE VAUDREY. Silence! Ah, Henriette!

(Enter HENRIETTE *hurriedly and weeping. She throws herself upon a chair, at table.)*

HENRIETTE *(weeping)*. Shame! Shame! I am sure I do not deserve to be so insulted.

DE VAUDREY. Who has insulted you?

HENRIETTE. I am ordered to leave this house.

DE VAUDREY. Ordered to leave this house! Why?

HENRIETTE. Alas! Monsieur, they tell me that a young girl living alone has not the right to receive the visits of gentlemen such as you.

DE VAUDREY. Such as I—I who have always treated you with the respect due a sister!

PICARD *(aside)*. Just now she was his wife—now she is his sister! Oh, it's all right.

HENRIETTE. The mistress of the house, who until now has been so kind to me, says she cannot permit me to remain, for she has a good name to protect, which my conduct scandalizes.

PICARD. Poor thing! Monsieur, I say this is unjust, this—is—

DE VAUDREY. Shameful!

PICARD *(to* HENRIETTE*)*. Certainly, it is shameful! Mamselle, I will go to see that woman myself. I'll tell her you are not—

*(*HENRIETTE *looks up astonished; he becomes abashed and stammers.)*

That is—I mean that you—that he—that—I don't know what I mean.

DE VAUDREY. Henriette, dry your tears! You shall leave this house to enter mine! Not mine alone, but yours as well, for you shall enter it on the arm of your husband!

HENRIETTE. Your wife! No! No! That is impossible. Think of the immeasurable distance which separates us. How can I defy the will of your family? They are rich and powerful—a marriage with me would entail their enmity.

DE VAUDREY. If my family will not *give* their consent, I will find means to compel them.

PICARD *(very energetically)*. Certainly—we'll compel them!

DE VAUDREY. Picard, my hat, we must go!

*(*PICARD *gets hat and hands it to him.)*

PICARD. Yes, monsieur, we must go.

DE VAUDREY. Henriette, I go to find the means of assuring our happiness!

HENRIETTE. Farewell, monsieur, farewell!

DE VAUDREY. No, Henriette, I will not say farewell. I cannot part with all my hopes. I need them to give me courage—au revoir!

HENRIETTE *(gives her hand and forces herself to smile).* Au revoir! *(Exit* PICARD *and* DE VAUDREY. HENRIETTE *throws herself on a chair.)*

No, I have not the strength to continue this conflict between love and duty. I am justly punished. Insulted, driven from this house. I must go where I shall never see him again!

(During the last lines, she rises and begins to search for her things as though preparing to go. Knock is heard and the door opens. Enter COUNTESS LEVANT.*)*

COUNTESS. Mademoiselle Henriette de Gaul, I believe.

HENRIETTE *(surprised).* That is my name, madame.

COUNTESS. You have been warmly recommended to me, mademoiselle.

HENRIETTE. Recommended to you, madame?

COUNTESS. Yes, I am the Countess Levant. I have known for some time the attachment which exists between you and my nephew, and I have defended him against the wrath of my husband. But reflection has shown me my duty to you both. The opposition of his family renders this marriage impossible.

HENRIETTE. Madame, I had determined my course before seeing you. The path of sacrifice and duty.

COUNTESS. I shall not prove ungrateful. I am rich and powerful.

HENRIETTE *(looking up, interested).* Powerful?

COUNTESS. And if at any time I can show my appreciation of your noble conduct—

HENRIETTE. Madame, you can; now—at this very instant—you can.

COUNTESS. How?

HENRIETTE. Use your power to find the poor child who has been torn from my protection. Do I ask too much?

COUNTESS. No, no. I promise you not alone my aid, but that of the greatest power in Paris. Give me her name, her age and description.

HENRIETTE. A description, alas, madame, too easily given. She is but sixteen and blind!

COUNTESS. Blind?

HENRIETTE. Her name is Louise.

COUNTESS *(with feeling).* Louise! That name is very dear to me. Be comforted, my child, we will find your sister.

HENRIETTE. She is not my sister, Madame.

COUNTESS. Not your sister?

HENRIETTE. No, madame, but I owe her the love and tenderness of a mother and sister combined, for she saved us all from misery and want.

COUNTESS. How could a poor child do that?

HENRIETTE. From poverty so terrible that my father had not even bread to give us. Anxious to save at least the life of his child, he took me and set out toward Notre Dame. There he stood weeping and irresolute, when suddenly he heard a plaintive cry. He approached and saw a babe half buried under the snow. He took her to his breast to warm her, when the thought came to him that, as this child would have died had he not arrived in time to save it, so his own might die before help could reach her. "I will leave neither of them," he said, and he returned carrying both infants in his arms.

COUNTESS. Oh! Go on, mademoiselle, go on.

HENRIETTE. Entering his home, he said to my mother, "We had only one child, Heaven has sent us another." Heaven rewarded his generous action, for on opening the clothing of the child, a roll of gold was found, with these words written on a scrap of paper, "Her name is Louise, save her."

COUNTESS *(struggling with herself)*. Ah!

HENRIETTE *(astonished)*. Are you ill, madame?

COUNTESS *(trying to be calm)*. No! No! I—it is nothing! Then the infant fell among good and worthy people?

HENRIETTE. Ah, madame, I cannot tell you how we loved her.

COUNTESS. Now I know why Maurice loves you. I will love you, too!

HENRIETTE. Then you will help me to find her?

COUNTESS *(with force)*. Help you? *(Rises.)* All Paris shall be searched from end to end. *(Crosses.)* But—she is blind! How is that? And how did you lose her? Tell me all.

(The voice of LOUISE *is heard faintly at a great distance, gradually approaching. As* HENRIETTE *speaks, she grows more abstracted, listening to the voice.)*

HENRIETTE. Yes, madame—it—was—one evening—

COUNTESS. Go on—my child—

HENRIETTE *(listening)*. About—about two years ago.

COUNTESS. Two years ago. Well?

HENRIETTE. Yes, two years ago. Louise was then—

COUNTESS *(astonished at the abstraction of* HENRIETTE*)*. Go on.

HENRIETTE. Louise was then—fourteen.

(Voice approaches nearer.)

We were playing together one evening, when—

(Voice is now quite close under the window; HENRIETTE *screams.)*

Ah!

COUNTESS. What is it?

HENRIETTE. Hush—sh, listen! It is she, madame, it is she! *(Rushes to the window.)*

COUNTESS. She? The poor little beggar whom I just left on the steps of the church?

LOUISE *(outside, after finishing her song)*. Henriette! Henriette! Do you hear me?

HENRIETTE. Louise! I am coming. I am coming!

LOUISE *(outside)*. It is I, Louise, your sister! *(Then cries out as though she had been checked.)* Ah!

HENRIETTE *(frightened).* Ah, what is that?

COUNTESS. Come, come!

(As they reach the door, it is violently thrown open and LEVANT *enters, followed by an* OFFICER. COUNTESS *stops suddenly.)*

My husband!

HENRIETTE. Gentlemen, gentlemen, do not stop me!

LEVANT *(to* OFFICER*).* Do your duty!

*(*OFFICER *seizes her.)*

HENRIETTE. In the name of heaven, let me go! Take pity! Let me go or I shall lose her again!

LEVANT. Take this girl to prison!

HENRIETTE *(screams).* Ah! No! No!

*(*OFFICER *takes her out, struggling.)*

COUNTESS *(tries to go out).* At least let me go! I must go!

LEVANT *(takes her by the arm).* You will remain where you are, madame. You have not told me what brought you here.

COUNTESS. Later, monsieur, I will tell you everything. But now let me go before she—

COUNT. Of whom are you speaking, madame?

COUNTESS. Of—of—of—my—

*(*LEVANT *looks at her sternly and threateningly. She screams and faints.)*

Ah!

(The voice of LOUISE *is heard faintly in the distance.)*

CURTAIN

The Count Levant detains his wife in Henriette's room after she has discovered that the blind orphan Louise is her daughter. VanAnn Moore plays the Countess; John Masterman plays her husband, the Count Levant, Minister of Police.

ACT THREE

SCENE ONE

SCENE: *Prison courtyard surrounded by leafless trees. At back, a wall, over which can be seen the dome of a church. There is a grated gate in the wall, a door leading to dormitory, a door to the hospital. Several prisoners are discovered kneeling in prayer with* SISTER GENEVIEVE, *Sister Superior of the Hospital. She is dressed in a nun's habit with hood. The gate opens and* DOCTOR *enters,* SISTER GENEVIEVE *rises, dismisses the girls who exit into dormitory.*

SISTER G. Ah, Doctor, I have been waiting impatiently for you.

DOCTOR *(looking at his watch).* I am not late, I believe.

SISTER G. No, but you led me to hope that when you came today you would bring me —

DOCTOR. Good news? Yes. Well, I have done everything in my power. I have spoken of the interest you take in this unfortunate woman, of her sincere repentance.

SISTER G. Then you have succeeded?

DOCTOR. Completely!

SISTER G. Ah, Heaven be praised! *(Calling.)* Jeanette, come here, my child!

JEAN *(coming in from dormitory).* Do you want me, Sister?

SISTER G. Yes, hurry, we cannot keep the doctor waiting. Here is the good doctor, who will tell you what he has done for you.

JEAN. For me?

DOCTOR. You must thank Sister Genevieve, not me. Touched by your repentance, she has solicited and obtained your pardon and release.

*(*DOCTOR *hands two official papers to* SISTER GENEVIEVE.*)*

JEAN. My benefactress! My Mother!

DOCTOR. No, your release is granted to the good Sister Genevieve. To that good and noble woman, who, born within the walls of this prison, has never consented to cross its threshold; who has made this prison her country and its unfortunate inmates her family; who brings to you all her daily blessings of consolation and prayer, so that even the vilest here respect and love her.

*(*JEANETTE *kneels and kisses* SISTER GENEVIEVE's *hand.)*
I did not intend to make you weep, Jeanette. Come, come, I shall be crying, too, in a minute. *(He helps her to her feet.)*

(Bell is heard striking.)

SISTER. It is time to go in. Come, my child. This evening you will be free. *(Gives her one of the documents which the* DOCTOR *brought.)* Do not forget that I am responsible for you. Society sent me a guilty woman; I return it a repentant one, I hope, Jeanette.

JEAN. I hope so, Sister. *(Loud noise is heard outside in the hospital.)*

HENRIETTE *(outside).* Leave me, leave me! Let me go!

SISTER. What is the meaning of those cries?

(HENRIETTE *appears at door, held by policeman with whom she is* *struggling.)*

HENRIETTE. You shall not keep me! I must go! I tell you I must!

JEAN *(looking at her).* Good heavens! *(Goes up.)*

HENRIETTE *(runs to* SISTER GENEVIEVE*).* Oh, madame! If you are mistress here, have pity on me! Order them to set me free! I ask you on my knees!

SISTER *(gently).* Be calm, my child. You are ill.

DOCTOR. Certainly you are. Why have you left your bed without my permission?

HENRIETTE. But, monsieur, I am well now. Now that you see I am quite well, you will tell them to let me go, will you not?

DOCTOR. That is impossible. To release you from this place requires a far greater power than mine.

HENRIETTE. This place? Why, what is it? Is it not a hospital?

DOCTOR. A hospital and a prison.

HENRIETTE. A prison! Ah, I remember. Yes, I remember the soldiers who dragged me thither, and he who commanded them. "To the Hospital of La Salpetriere," he said, the prison for *(Looking round her.)* unfortunate women. Oh! My God! *(Goes to bench at back and weeps.)*

DOCTOR *(to* SISTER GENEVIEVE*).* Sister, this is not a case for my care. You must be the physician here. *(Crosses and exits into hospital.)*

SISTER. I have seen many guilty women, but this one —

JEAN. Is not guilty, Sister.

SISTER. Do you know her?

JEAN. When I came here, I told you that on that very day I had been prevented from adding the crime of suicide to my many sins by two young girls, angels of virtue and goodness. This is one of them.

SISTER. How is it possible that she should be here?

JEAN. Misfortunes may have overtaken her, but I am sure that vice has never sullied her life.

(PICARD *appears at the gate, speaks with* SISTER GENEVIEVE *and shows her a paper. After a few words, he is admitted.* JEANETTE *goes to* HENRIETTE *and brings her forward.)*

SISTER. Courage, my child. Look up.

JEAN. Look at me, mademoiselle. Do you not know me? Do you not remember the woman who wished to drown herself?

HENRIETTE *(looking up slowly).* You — you? Ah, yes, I remember you too well. *(Despairingly.)* Alas! We were together then. You saw her, my poor sister.

SISTER. By whose orders were you sent here?

PICARD *(comes down).* By the order of the Count Levant, madame.

SISTER. Who are you, sir?

PICARD *(with importance).* First valet-de-chambre to his Excellency, the Minister of Police.

SISTER. Then it is by his order that this poor child is —

PICARD. Alas! Madame, the honor of an illustrious house must be protected.

HENRIETTE. You are witness that I refused the hand of the Baron De Vaudrey!

PICARD. If Madame the Superior will allow me to inform the young lady of the further wishes of His Excellency the Minister of Police, I think I can make her understand.

SISTER. You may do so. *(To* HENRIETTE.*)* Have courage, my child, trust in heaven. *(Kisses her on forehead, crosses. To* JEANETTE.*)* Jeanette!

*(*JEANETTE *precedes her as they exit D.R.)*

HENRIETTE. We are alone. What new misery do you bring me?

PICARD. Come, come, mademoiselle—can you never forgive me? That is too bad, to have you reproach me, too. Because the master I deceive is the Minister of Police.

HENRIETTE. But Baron De Vaudrey, what of him?

PICARD. He refused to obey his uncle, and—and yesterday he was sent to prison, too.

HENRIETTE. He too is a prisoner, then?

PICARD. Yes—he made me swear to come here and tell you that if, at the worst, they decided to send you into exile to Cayenne—

HENRIETTE. Exile! Cayenne! Why, that would be death!

PICARD *(in an undertone).* Wait a little, mamselle. If my pretended master comes to that decision, he will release my real master from prison, and once he gets out of there, why, off he goes, followed by your humble servant. We overtake the guard having you in charge. With the gold with which we take care to be provided, my real master will bribe the guards, and if they should be incorruptible, that is, if we have not enough money with us to buy them, why, then we will share your exile, and we will be happy in spite of the treachery of my other master.

HENRIETTE. You speak to me of happiness? Who then will search for my sister, Louise?

PICARD. Do I count for nothing? Do you suppose that a member of the secret police of His Excellency the Minister of Police is going to fold his arms quietly? No—come, come, mademoiselle, I will arrange everything.

*(*OFFICER *appears at gate.* SISTER GENEVIEVE *enters with* JEANETTE *and opens gate.)*

HENRIETTE *(pointing to* OFFICER*).* Good heavens! Look there!

OFFICER. Sister Superior, I have the honor to hand you this list of prisoners, who by the order of His Excellency the Minister of Police, are condemned to exile. Permit me to order them assembled here and we can proceed to identify them. *(Hands papers to* SISTER GENEVIEVE.*)*

SISTER. You may do so, monsieur. I will follow you.

*(*OFFICER *salutes and exits.)*

The list! I dread to look at it. *(She opens the paper hesitatingly, and reads. Looks at* HENRIETTE, *and cries out.)* Ah!

HENRIETTE. Madame, why do you look at me so? Answer me, for pity's sake! Have mercy!

SISTER. Ah, my poor child!

HENRIETTE. I see it. Alas! I am condemned. I am lost, lost!

(Enter DOCTOR.*)*

PICARD *(aside to* SISTER GENEVIEVE*)*. Madame, is this true?

SISTER *(showing the list)*. Henriette de Gaul.

(HENRIETTE *screams and falls weeping into the arms of the* DOC-TOR *and* JEANETTE, *who led her to the bench.* SISTER GENEVIEVE *stops and looks at her pityingly for a moment and exits.)*

PICARD. They are going to send her off immediately. Today! I will go to the prison and inform the Baron, my master, that my other master has villainously deceived me—that he has had the indelicacy to actually suspect my fidelity. Ah! He shall pay for that!

HENRIETTE *(to* JEANETTE, *coming forward)*. Ah! Now I understand why one may wish to die!

JEAN. Do not speak so, Mademoiselle. Remember the words of hope you spoke to me.

HENRIETTE *(to* DOCTOR*)*. Ah! sir, exile has no terrors for me. I do not weep for my own misfortunes, but for my sister's. I had found her at the moment they arrested me. I heard her voice; I saw her. She was covered with rags. She was being dragged along by a horrible old woman, who I know ill-treats her, beats her, perhaps.

DOCTOR *(trying to recall)*. Wait a minute, my child. I believe that I have met that very young girl.

HENRIETTE. You, monsieur?

DOCTOR. Yes, yes. A young girl led by an old woman who called her Louise.

HENRIETTE. Yes, yes; that is her name!

DOCTOR. I know the old woman, too; she is called La Frochard.

PICARD. La Frochard? The old hag who goes about whining for alms in the name of Heaven and seven poor children. Where does she live?

JEAN *(aside)*. Jacques' mother! She must be saved from their vile hands. *(Aloud)*. She lives in a hovel by the river side; it was formerly used as a boathouse, but has long been occupied by thieves and the worst criminals. There is a secret entrance from the Rue Noir, but it is difficult to find, and it is always carefully guarded.

PICARD. Never mind that. The police of Paris can find secret en-trances. If not, we'll capture the main one. First to release my master—then for the boathouse! *(Exit.)*

HENRIETTE. You are sure she lives there? Then we will go at once. I have found her again. *(Recollects herself, utters a cry.)* Ah! I am to be sent away, away far from her.

JEAN. No, no, mademoiselle—you need not—you shall not be sent away. *(To* DOCTOR.*)* Doctor, have pity on her and consent to help me.

(Enter OFFICER.*)*

OFFICER. I need another prisoner to complete the list, Henriette De Gaul.

JEAN *(advances very quickly to* OFFICER*)*. Here, monsieur.

HENRIETTE *(low)*. Ahhh!

DOCTOR *(seizes her arm)*. Silence!

JEAN *(to* OFFICER*)*. Permit me, monsieur, to bid her a last farewell!
*(*OFFICER *makes gesture of consent and exits.* JEANETTE *crosses to* HENRIETTE*.)*

HENRIETTE. No, no! I cannot, I will not consent!

JEAN. Hush! It is not you whom I save, Henriette, it is myself. If I remain, Jacques will find me again, and once in his power I shall be lost. You will remain, you will find Louise, and we will both be saved.

HENRIETTE. Louise?

JEAN. Here, take this.
*(*JEANETTE *gives* HENRIETTE *the paper which* SISTER GENEVIEVE *has given her.* HENRIETTE *hesitates and looks at* DOCTOR*.)*

DOCTOR *(behind* HENRIETTE*)*. Take it. Your sister's fate depends upon it.
*(*HENRIETTE *takes the paper and embraces* JEANETTE, *weeping. Enter* SISTER GENEVIEVE *and* OFFICER*.)*
Ah—the Sister Superior!

OFFICER *(to* SISTER GENEVIEVE*)*. Madame, will you please verify this list and identify the prisoners who are intended for exile?

SISTER. I am ready, monsieur!

OFFICER *(reading from list)*. Marie Morand?
(As each name is called, one of the girls comes from hospital, head down, face averted. SISTER GENEVIEVE *looks into the face of each one as they pass.)*

SISTER. Yes.

OFFICER. Jeanne Raymond?

SISTER. Yes.

OFFICER *(turning to* JEANETTE*)*. Henriette de Gaul?

JEAN. Here, Mother! *(Crosses to* SISTER GENEVIEVE *and kneels.)*

SISTER. You?
*(*DOCTOR *points to* HENRIETTE *with appealing gesture.* SISTER GENEVIEVE *looks from one to the other and seems greatly agitated.)*

JEAN. Mother! Mother! Have pity, Bless me and let me go, for this exile will purify a guilty soul and save an innocent one.

OFFICER. Well, Sister?
*(*SISTER GENEVIEVE *takes* JEANETTE's *head in her hands, stoops and kisses her forehead, and then, with a firm voice and eyes uplifted to heaven.)*

SISTER. Yes. *(Aside.)* Ah, Doctor—my first falsehood.

TABLEAU

CURTAIN

In the prison "La Salpetriere," Jeanette volunteers to take Henriette's place as one of the prisoners sent into exile at Cayenne. Sister Genevieve verifies the falsehood, as she silently asks Heaven's forgiveness. Jeanne Miclot is Henriette; Sheila Stanker, Jeanette; Nancy Holt, Sister Genevieve; and Herb Prizeman, the Officer.

SCENE TWO

SCENE: *The hut of* LA FROCHARD. *The stage represents an old and dilapidated boathouse. At the back C. are two large and heavy doors opening down, which are closed with a bar across resting in heavy socket and secured by padlock. Beyond doors, when they are forced open, are discovered steps leading down to the river. Across river can be seen views of Paris by starlight. At L. is a staircase leading up to a garret with door opening down. Door has lock and bolt. In room is a crude bed, a table with knife-grinding machine. At rise of curtain,* LOUISE *and* PIERRE *are discovered,* LOUISE *asleep upon miserable straw bed,* PIERRE *seated on stool at foot of bed.*

PIERRE. Poor child! So young, so weak, so lovely, and yet condemned to so hard a fate. Ah—and I can do nothing. Jacques suspects and watches me. If I were to make a step toward her release, Jacques would discover it and kill me. *(He rises and looks at her.)* Ah—she shivers in her sleep, she must be ill!

LOUISE *(half rising).* Who is there?

PIERRE. It is I—mamselle, Pierre!

LOUISE. Ah, Pierre! I am glad it is you. I may sleep a little longer, may I not?

PIERRE. Sleep, mamselle, sleep—don't be frightened, I will not leave you.

LOUISE. I am so tired—thank you, Pierre, thank you. *(She lies down.)*

PIERRE *(looking at her).* Yes, sleep, poor child, and forget your misery. *(Pauses.)* Jacques has forbidden me to think of her, but I will think of her—aye—and save her, too, even if it costs me my life. I can weaken these bolts, and Jacques will not discover it. *(He goes to wheel, takes a screwdriver and works at screws in heavy bolt across the door.)* What am I doing? Alas! I shall pay for this with my life. No, no, I cannot!

LOUISE *(sighs in her sleep).* Henriette! Sister Henriette!

PIERRE *(running to her side).* She dreams of her sister—a smile lights her face. *(Thoughtfully.)* Ah! If I help her to escape and her happy dream were to become a reality, she might remember me with pity, perhaps with love. *(Goes up.)* I have begun my work and I will finish it.

*(*PIERRE *returns to doors at back and is about to commence work when* LA FROCHARD *enters from door under staircase.)*

FRO *(brings in carrot and turnip, which she puts on table and scrapes through dialogue which follows).* Hello, master knife-grinder! What brings you home so early? No work outside, eh?

PIERRE. It is growing dark. I have brought my work home with me.

FRO. So as to be near to Mamselle Louise. Oh, I have my eye on you.

PIERRE. It would be better to have your eye on Jacques. But you never find fault with him.

FRO. Why should I? He is the oldest, and master here.

(Enter JACQUES *by door under staircase.)*

JACQUES. There, that will do for today. *(Takes off apron and throws it.)* No more work for me. I'm tired of it. *(Crosses and sits on a stool.)*

FRO. It is tiresome, isn't it, my son?

JACQUES. Ugh! Disgusting. *(Sees* PIERRE.*)* Hello, Master Cupid. *(Looking at* LOUISE.*)* What is this? Asleep. Why isn't she at work?

FRO. That is what I want to know, sleeping instead of working for her living.

JACQUES *(looking at her).* Why, she is so used to it that she cries when she sleeps.

PIERRE *(looking at* LOUISE*).* Is she crying?

JACQUES *(stops him).* What's that to you?

FRO. She is obstinate, lazy and a hypocrite. This morning I had to push her along to make her walk at all, and as to singing, she has no more voice than a crow.

JACQUES *(sitting).* I will make her sing.

PIERRE. You will kill her. Can't you see she is ill?

FRO. Nonsense—she is shamming—I know her tricks.

JACQUES. What is the matter with her now?

FRO. She has got some new notion in her head—I can't tell what.

PIERRE. I can. You remember the night of the snowstorm. After finishing her song, she cried out at the top of her voice, "Henriette, my sister."

FRO. Yes, and I stopped her mouth pretty quick, too.

PIERRE. Yes, yes, you twisted her arm until you nearly broke it.

FRO. Well, why didn't she mind me?

PIERRE. You're killing her.

FRO. I can't afford to support her idleness. She has to work, and if she won't—

JACQUES. I'll find a way to make her sing—

PIERRE. You, what would you do?

JACQUES *(crossing to* PIERRE*).* That is my business.

FRO *(goes to* LOUISE*).* Come, get up, my fine lady. No more airs. You must go out and make your living.

(She makes LOUISE *rise.)*

Give me that shawl. *(Throws shawl on bed.)* Take off this scarf; it keeps you too warm. *(Takes off scarf and puts it on her own neck.)* You'll shiver more comfortably without it.

LOUISE. I don't wish to go out, madame.

FRO *(to* JACQUES*).* Eh? What next? You hear that? She don't wish to go out.

JACQUES. We'll see about that. *(Crosses to* LOUISE *and goes to take her hand.)* Come here, my little beauty.

LOUISE *(recoils from his touch).* I forbid *you* to touch me.

JACQUES. Oh, ho! Then we're no longer friends?

LOUISE. Friends? You? You're cruel wretches! Both of you.

Pierre sits by helplessly as his brother Jacques attempts to push the blind Louise out to beg once more. La Frochard looks on with admiration at her son's consistent cruelty and heartlessness. Lynn Bradley is the evil La Frochard; Allen Fearon, Pierre; Mary Stevens, Louise; and Joe Maltsberger is Jacques Frochard.

JACQUES. Yet you were glad enough to share our home when we picked you up in the streets.

LOUISE. Yes; I was grateful to you then, because you offered me shelter. Alas! I learned too soon it was not pity for my misfortune that moved you. No, no, you wanted to make use of my affliction. You have starved, tortured, *beaten* me; but now—weak as I am—my will shall be stronger than your violence! *(Straightening herself up.)* I will beg no more!

PIERRE *(terrified).* Louise!

JACQUES. Ah! When her blood is up, she is superb!

FRO. Oh, well, well, that is all mighty fine; but where is the bread and butter to come from?

LOUISE. I care not!

PIERRE *(crossing to* LA FROCHARD). Do you hear? Do you know what she means? She will starve rather than beg.

FRO. Nonsense, she will get tired of that soon enough.

LOUISE. Never!

FRO. Well, we'll see if locking you up in that garret won't bring you to your senses.

LOUISE. If I enter that place, you know I will never leave it alive.

JACQUES. Why, she is magnificent. I'd never have believed she had so much spirit. *(Advances towards her.)* Why—I love you! *(Seizes her and attempts to kiss her.)*

LOUISE. Ah! *(Screams and escapes from him.)*

PIERRE *(angrily).* Jacques! *(Loudly, coming down on his L.)*

JACQUES. Well, what is it? You don't like it, I suppose, Master Cupid. Well, forbid it, why don't you?

PIERRE. I do! *(Looks at* JACQUES *who eyes him sternly and he cowers U.)* Oh, miserable, cowardly wretch that I am! *(Breaks down sobbing, goes to wheel.)*

FRO *(crosses to* LOUISE). Come—come along. You're strong enough when you want to be. Up into the garret with you.

(She leads LOUISE *to the foot of the stairs.* LOUISE *falls on steps.)*

JACQUES. Yes, that is right, mother, take her up there out of the way. Here—I want to speak to you.

*(*LA FROCHARD *crosses to* JACQUES; *they whisper.)*

PIERRE *(going to* LOUISE, *at foot of steps, and speaking in a low tone, very rapidly).* You can escape, I have unscrewed the lock; the key to the door to the street is under your mattress. Trust to heaven to guide you. Nothing worse can happen than threatens you here.

JACQUES *(aloud to* LA FROCHARD). Lock her up securely. I have my reasons for distrusting Master Cupid here!

FRO. Yes, yes, I understand.

JACQUES. Come with me and keep your whining for this blind beauty till another time. Come along, I say!

(He pulls PIERRE *off R.)*

FRO *(sitting).* Ah! What a splendid fellow he is. The very image of his dear father. There was a man for you. They cut off his head. *(Turns to* LOUISE *and takes bottle from her pocket, from which she drinks.)* Ah! That warms my heart! *(To* LOUISE.*)* Yes, Jacques is right. We must break your obstinate spirit.

*(*LOUISE *has sunk down on steps.* LA FROCHARD *goes to her.)*

Ah! Shamming again. Get up and come with me!

*(*LA FROCHARD *forces her to rise and they go up the stairs.)*

LOUISE. Oh, Madame, have you no soul, no pity? Do not kill me!

FRO. I don't intend to. You're too valuable. There, get in with you. I'll see you safe inside.

(They exit into garret. LA FROCHARD *closes the door. After a moment's pause, the door under the stairs opens and* PICARD *enters.)*

PICARD. Ah! At last I've found a door that leads to something and somewhere. *(Looks about him.)* There's nobody at home! *(Sees brandy bottle, takes it up.)* Hello, what's this? Brandy! *(Smells it.)* Bad brandy; very bad brandy! What is my best course? Let me see. *(Examines C. doors.)* These doors must open on the river. Good. That is the point for the police. Now to return through the half-mile dark passages to the Rue Noir where I left Mamselle Henriette; then to the Baron, liberated by his uncle on the assumption that Mamselle Henriette has been sent to Cayenne. And now, if I have not earned my promotion, my name is not Picard. *(Exit understairs, slamming door.)*

(Enter LA FROCHARD.*)*

FRO *(opening door of garret).* Hm! Eh! What's that? *(Comes down quickly.)* I thought I heard someone. Jacques, is that you? No, there is no one here. I'm an old fool to be so easily frightened—it's my nerves. *(Drinks.)*

(Knock at door.)

Who's that?

(Knock heard again.)

Who can have found their way here? *(She hides the bottle and goes to the door.)* Who is there? What do you want?

HENRIETTE *(outside).* I am looking for someone—for Madame Frochard.

FRO. What do you want of her?

HENRIETTE *(outside).* I must speak with her.

FRO. Are you alone?

HENRIETTE. Yes, I am alone.

FRO *(cautiously opens the door and looks behind* HENRIETTE*).* Well, if you are alone, you may come in.

(Enter HENRIETTE *looking around her, affright.* LA FROCHARD *closes door and comes down.)*

HENRIETTE. How imprudent I was to leave the spot where Picard left me. I have lost him and wandered here by accident. Great heaven! Can this be the place?

FRO. Well, well, young woman, you want to see Madame Frochard.

What have you got to say to her? Do you expect to find anyone here?

HENRIETTE (*looks around searchingly*). Yes, yes, I am looking for the person who lives here with you.

FRO. What person?

HENRIETTE. A young girl.

FRO. I don't know anything about any young girl.

HENRIETTE (*astonished*). You don't know her?

FRO. No!

HENRIETTE. Am I mistaken? This house answers the description and your name is Frochard, is it not?

FRO. Euphemie Frochard—what then?

HENRIETTE (*Sees* LOUISE's *shawl on the bed and utters a loud cry*). Ah!

FRO. What is the matter?

HENRIETTE (*seizes the shawl*). This shawl! I know it—it is hers, it is hers, I tell you!

FRO. Not a bit of it. It is mine. (*Attempts to recover the shawl.*)

HENRIETTE. And the scarf around your neck?

FRO. Well, what of it?

HENRIETTE. It was made for her by my own hands. (*Tears the scarf from* LA FROCHARD's *neck.*) Ah, wretch, you have lied to me.

FRO. Well, well, if you must know the truth, I'll tell you. When you came in, you were so excited and frightened that I didn't dare tell you all—

HENRIETTE. What? Speak quickly.

FRO. One evening, about three months ago, I met the girl you are looking for wandering about in the streets. I had pity on her and brought her home with me, where I took good care of her. But you see, the poor child wasn't very strong, and what with the life we lead and the sorrow she felt, she could not stand it. She broke down entirely, and that was the end of it. For two days now she has been gone.

HENRIETTE. Dead! Louise—dead! (*She faints.*)

FRO. Ah! fainted. What am I to do with her? Oh, if Jacques were only here. I must go for him. But if she were to come to and see the other one. No, no, I'll fix that. (*She goes up the stairs, locks the garret door, takes the key with her.*) There, there is nothing to fear now; I'll go and call Jacques.

(*She exits at door L. and is heard to lock the door on the other side after her. As soon as she is off, the door of the garret is seen to move, at first gently, then with more force. Finally the lock tumbles off, the door opens and* LOUISE *appears.*)

LOUISE. They are all gone. Pierre told me the truth, the lock would not hold. (*She comes down.*) If I can find my way to the street, through that long passage—(*She gropes around and passes very close to* HENRIETTE.) Where is the door? Ah, here. (*She tries the door L.*) Locked, locked; what shall I do? Ah—I remember, Pierre told me he had made another key for it. (*She gropes her way rapidly to the bed, feels under the mattress and finds the key.)* Ah, good, brave Pierre, now I will go at once. *(She crosses the stage with rapid steps and stumbles against* HENRIETTE. *She recoils frightened, then advances and stoops, feeling with her hands.)* A woman! *(She touches* HENRIETTE's *hand.)* Oh, Heaven! They have committed some horrible crime and fled. *(She raises* HENRIETTE's *head to her knees and puts her hand on her heart.)* Madame, madame, speak, speak to me.

> *(The door is heard to unlock and* LA FROCHARD *and* JACQUES *enter quickly.)*

FRO. How is this? Together!

JACQUES. Separate them at once—quick!

FRO *(dragging* LOUISE *away from* HENRIETTE*)*. What are you doing here? How did you get out?

LOUISE. I—madame—I!

JACQUES *(seeing* HENRIETTE *recovering)*. Quick, get her out of the way—quick, I tell you—the other one is coming to.

> *(*PIERRE *appears at door.)*

LOUISE. But this woman who is lying here!

> *(At that moment* HENRIETTE *opens her eyes and sees* LOUISE.*)*

HENRIETTE *(screams)*. Louise! Louise!

> *(*JACQUES *puts his hand over her mouth.)*

LOUISE *(stops)*. That voice? I know it.

FRO. Go on—I tell you—get in with you!

HENRIETTE *(pushing* JACQUES' *hand away)*. Louise! Sister!

> *(With an effort,* LOUISE *pushes* LA FROCHARD *aside and runs down the stairs.* HENRIETTE *disengages herself from* JACQUES. *They meet C. and embrace.)*

LOUISE. Henriette! Henriette! It is you!

HENRIETTE. Louise, Louise! My sister!

PIERRE *(joyfully)*. Her sister! She has found her! Now I would gladly die—now that she is happy.

HENRIETTE. Oh, my Louise, my poor Louise! What have they done to you? Miserable wretches that you are! I will have you punished.

> *(*JACQUES *goes to door L.)*

Let us go at once! Let us go!

JACQUES *(barring the passage)*. No, you shall not go! You cannot leave here.

HENRIETTE. I will cry out—I will call for help!

JACQUES *(backing them to R.)* Try it, and see what good it will do! Besides, I warn you we come of a family that kills! *(Seizes* LOUISE, *dragging both of them to C.)* She is mine and I will keep her!

LOUISE *(screams)*. Ah!

> *(*PIERRE *rushes in between* LOUISE *and* JACQUES, *forcing* JACQUES *to release* LOUISE, *and he faces* JACQUES.*)*

JACQUES. You dare to interfere against me?

PIERRE. I dare!

JACQUES. Against me!

PIERRE. Against you! I have acted the coward long enough. I thought, because you were big and strong, that you were brave—but you are not! You fight women—you are a coward! In their defense, my courage will be more than a match for your strength!

LOUISE. Brave Pierre!

JACQUES *(advancing to him)*. What do you want?

PIERRE. Let these two women go!

JACQUES. Indeed! Suppose I refuse, what then?

PIERRE. What then? What then? Well, you have said it—we come from a family that kills.

FRO *(on steps)*. Pierre!

PIERRE. Lay a hand on either of them *(Runs to his wheel and takes up knife.)* and I plunge this knife into your heart.

(JACQUES recoils as though in spite of himself.)

JACQUES. Your life shall pay for this!

PIERRE. Or yours!

FRO. Remember you are brothers!

PIERRE *(bitterly)*. Yes, brothers—the sons of Adam—only this time Abel will kill Cain!

JACQUES. Very well, if you will have it.

(He takes knife from PIERRE; they fight, and JACQUES wounds PIERRE in the shoulder.)

HENRIETTE. He is wounded.

PIERRE. No!

JACQUES. Isn't that enough, cripple?

PIERRE. No; cut again, for while she is in danger, you may slash my flesh to ribbons. I shall feel nothing.

(They fight again. PIERRE wrests knife from JACQUES and stabs him. He falls dead. PIERRE stares at him in horror.)

Yes, he was right, we do come of a family that kills!

FRO *(crossing to PIERRE in fury)*. And for this, I shall kill you! You have killed my strong, handsome son, and you shall pay with your worthless life!

(During this speech she takes knife from PIERRE who gives it up without a struggle. HENRIETTE comes forward.)

HENRIETTE. No! No!

(As LA FROCHARD raises knife to stab PIERRE, door is thrust open violently. DE VAUDREY enters, grabs LA FROCHARD and takes knife away from her.)

DE VAUDREY. What's this? Would you kill this one who stands here defenseless?

FRO. Who are you to interfere? He is my miserable, misshapen son—and he has killed my handsome Jacques! *(Screams.)* I will kill him—I will!

(She attacks PIERRE. DE VAUDREY pulls her away and protects PIERRE.)

HENRIETTE. Oh, sir, you have come just in time—this lying hag would have killed us all!

(Noise is heard beyond door and voice of PICARD.*)*

PICARD. Open, open in the name of the law!

(The noise of a battering ram is heard against the door. The bar falls; doors open and enter PICARD *with* OFFICER *with drawn pistols.)*

PICARD. Ah, master, thank Heaven you are here!

DE VAUDREY. Yes, and in good time, Picard! Murder has been done here, and but for me, the old woman would have committed yet another! Officer—take that boy to prison!

LOUISE. No, no, he deserves no punishment! He killed in self-defense! But for him I should not be alive—he has been my only hope, my only defender against these evil ones! They have starved me, and only Pierre stood against them!

DE VAUDREY. My uncle, the Minister of Police will decide his fate, Henriette—but for now, he must go to prison.

PIERRE *(to* LOUISE*)*. Do not grieve, mamselle. I shall not mind, now that you are saved. *(To* OFFICER.*)* I will go with you.

(During this speech, LA FROCHARD *attempts to escape unnoticed. When she has almost reached door,* PICARD *wheels and catches her.)*

PICARD. Ah, no, you don't get off so easily, old woman! You shall go with your son and answer for your crimes.

FRO *(turning to audience)*. Charity—charity, good people, for a poor old woman—please—have pity on a poor mother with seven children at home.

*(PICARD *motions to* OFFICER, *who grabs* LA FROCHARD *and drags her off, kicking, biting and cursing. As he leaves,* OFFICER *calls to* PIERRE.)*

OFFICER. Come along, you!

PIERRE. I will come. *(To* LOUISE; *he takes her hand.)* Farewell, mamselle.

LOUISE *(weeping)*. Oh, dear, dear Pierre—*(She kisses him on cheek.)* I promise we will make them understand how brave you are!

*(OFFICER *calls from outside.)*

OFFICER. I say there—come along!

PIERRE *(as he joins* OFFICER *at exit)*. Brave—she said I was brave!

DE VAUDREY. Henriette, my love!

HENRIETTE. A second time I owe my life to you! Louise, my darling sister, thank your preserver.

LOUISE. Ah, monsieur, you do not know from what a frightful fate you have saved us!

DE VAUDREY *(to* PICARD*)*. And now, monsieur le capitaine, how are we to get away from this hole of a place?

PICARD. Monsieur le Baron, I have provided for everything. The Minister of Police promised to follow me here, with your aunt, the Countess, as soon as possible.

HENRIETTE. The Minister of Police coming here? Let me go with my poor Louise at once.

DE VAUDREY. Stay, Henriette! I have restored your sister to your arms, to replace your care by the endearing protection of a mother.

(The COUNT LEVANT, COUNTESS *and* DOCTOR *enter.)*

HENRIETTE *(bewildered)*. Mother?

LOUISE *(joyfully)*. My mother!

*(*DE VAUDREY *meets* COUNTESS *and brings her down.)*

DE VAUDREY. Your mother, the Countess de Levant.

COUNTESS *(embracing her)*. My child, my Louise!

HENRIETTE *(sadly)*. I have found her, only to lose her again!

LEVANT. Not so, mademoiselle. It is only within the past hour that I have learned the truth. The Countess has confessed the secret which has clouded our married life!

DE VAUDREY. Picard, you may unpack my trunks. I shall not go to Cayenne.

PICARD. No necessity for it, monsieur. We found our Cayenne in Paris, and for a few minutes as hot as we wanted it.

*(*COUNTESS *comes down with* LOUISE *and* HENRIETTE. PICARD *and* LEVANT *are engaged in whispering through the last two lines.)*

LOUISE. Monsieur, we are all so happy; yet you must not forget poor Pierre. Noble, brave Pierre!

COUNT. My dear, I promise you we shall not forget Pierre! If what Picard has told me is true, he will be pardoned.

LOUISE. Oh, I could never thank you enough. Henriette, how can we ever reward these kindnesses?

DE VAUDREY *(to* HENRIETTE*)*. Henriette, is my reward to be delayed longer?

HENRIETTE. To be near Louise, my sister, and to be your wife, seems too great a joy.

LOUISE *(to* COUNTESS*)*. Ah, mother, if I could only see you!

DOCTOR. Ah! That is my affair.

COUNTESS. And do you think you can restore her sight, doctor?

DOCTOR. I can be the instrument! The rest is in the hands of heaven!

TABLEAU TO HEAVEN

AND

CURTAIN

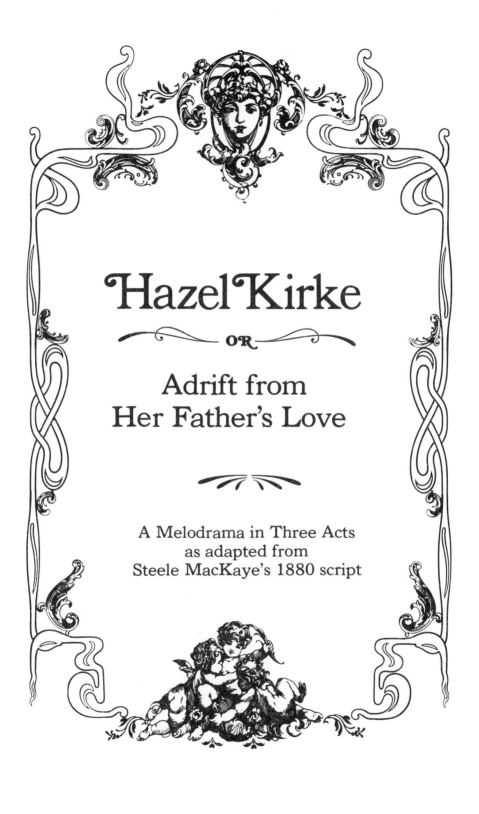

Hazel Kirke

OR

Adrift from
Her Father's Love

A Melodrama in Three Acts
as adapted from
Steele MacKaye's 1880 script

CAST OF CHARACTERS

DUNSTAN KIRKE, a dour Scottish miller
MERCY KIRKE, his wife
HAZEL KIRKE, their daughter
DOLLY DUTTON, Hazel's cousin
MET MIGGINS, an orphan girl in the care of the Kirke family
AARON RODNEY, country gentleman and friend of Dunstan Kirke
PITTACUS GREEN, who was born a baby
ARTHUR CARRINGFORD, a young lord (Lord Travers)
EMILY CARRINGFORD (Lady Travers), his mother
BARNEY O'FLYNN, Lord Travers' valet
JOE, mill hand
INSPECTOR, from Scotland Yard

SYNOPSIS OF SCENES

Time: Early spring, 1880   Place: Lancashire

ACT ONE

Exterior of Blackburn Mill.
          "Stand back, she is lost to thee forever!"

ACT TWO

LORD TRAVERS' villa at Fairy Grove.
          "May Heaven forgive you all."

ACT THREE

Scene One: The Kitchen of Blackburn Mill, evening.
          "Oh, God, this is thy punishment!"

Scene Two: Same, the following morning.
          "Peace after pain, and after sadness, mirth."

Then, as now, actors and actresses often found their metier in a given role and wished to continue playing it for long periods of time. Effie Ellsler played Hazel Kirke with Charles Couldock as Dunstan in the first New York production in 1880. They repeated their success in San Francisco in 1881.

About the Play

Hazel Kirke, under its earlier title, *An Iron Will*, was first produced at Low's Opera House in Providence, Rhode Island, on October 27, 1879, and subsequently it was taken on tour to Philadelphia, Baltimore, Washington and other cities. The first New York production took place on February 4, 1880 at the Madison Square Theatre, where Charles Couldock created the role of the dour Scotsman, Dunstan Kirke, and Effie Ellsler played the title role. The play proved very popular, with 486 performances during the first run in New York, followed by 1,500 with a travelling troupe.

Although the play continued to enjoy phenomenal success for close to 30 years, the playwright received only a salary of $5,000 for two years, during which time the profits amounted to $200,000. Miss Ellsler and Charles Couldock starred again in an 1881 production at the California Theatre in San Francisco. The famed Laurette Taylor appeared in a later revival at the New Third Avenue Theatre in Seattle, Washington, in September of 1907.

In the 1954 production of Hazel Kirke, *Met Miggins (Isabel McClung, far right) delivered the coup de grace as she hit Aaron Rodney (Dieter Kiebel) and rendered him senseless in the final scene. Watching are (left to right) Pittacus Green (Tom Rea), Dolly (Norma Loy), Mercy (Beth White), Arthur (Bill McCarthy) and Hazel (Shirley Strain).*

ACT ONE

SCENE: *Exterior of Blackburn, Dunstan Kirke's mill. At R., the exterior of house opens onto a courtyard. At L. is a large gateway. The walls to the courtyard are covered with vines. There is a view of the mill-wheel in the background. D.R. stands a bench; D.L., a rustic table with two chairs. A pile of empty bags is U.C., a broom on the porch. As the curtain rises,* JOE, *a mill hand in his forties, is discovered marking bags for market and* MET MIGGINS, *an orphan girl of about 25, is blowing a musical pipe.* JOE *is dressed in rough workman's clothing,* MET *in somber dress with scarf over her hair.*

DUNSTAN *(offstage).* Hey there, Dan, watch where you're loading that grain! *(He appears behind wall.)* Joe, you dolt, more bags, more bags! We hadn't got all day. *(Disappearing behind wall.)* Be off, boys, and bring another cart 'round. Will ye move your curs'd hides and look alive!

> *(Ad-lib from others offstage: "We're hurryin' as good as we kin." —"I can't find no more bags."—"Whoa, hold still, will ye?"*

MET *(mimicking Dunstan).* More bags—more bags for market!

JOE. Drat it! Give me time to mark 'em, can't ye?

MET *(blowing her pipe).* Oh, I don't care how long ye take, but old man Kirke is gettin' into one of his tempers.

JOE. Oh, his tempers be hanged! I'm doin' my best, no man can do more. *(He stands.)* Met Miggins—if you don't stop blowin' that frightful pipe o' yours, I'm goin' t' take the stick to ye!

MET. You wouldn't dare! If Miss Hazel found out, she'd see you off this place, and then where'd you go?

DUNSTAN *(offstage).* Hoorry, you dolts, or we'll never get loaded!

JOE *(to Met).* Seems to me y'd be a bit less ornery considerin' all Maister Kirke's done for ye since y' kin had the impudence t' die and leave you homeless. Y've growed up the mischievous booby ye are, and nobody c'n do a thing with ye, 'cept Mistress Hazel.

DUNSTAN *(offstage).* Hi there, Joe! Are ye never coomin' with those bags?

JOE. Aye—I'm coomin'! Drat that miller. If he don' beat the devil hisself. *(To Met.)* I'm warnin' ye, girl; bein' an orphan don' give ye the right to run 'round here like a half-wit mountain goat!

DUNSTAN *(offstage).* Are ye never coomin', ye lazy dolt?

MET *(teasing Joe).* You better hurry, Joe, or we'll all be killed. *(Starts blowing pipe again.)*

JOE. Ahh—h! You're as loony as they coom! *(yelling offstage.)* I'm coomin', I'm coomin'!

> *(Exit* JOE *U.L.* MET *follows blowing pipe). Enter* MERCY KIRKE *U.R. A Scottish country woman, middle-aged, in working dress with apron and mob-cap, she speaks with a thick accent.)*

MERCY. Dolly! Dolly, child!

DOLLY *(inside).* Aye, aye, aunt.

MERCY. Hoorry! Bring the bundles for market into the courtyard, lass.

DUNSTAN *(offstage)*. Bags, more bags, Joe!

JOE. Here ye are, I'm bringin' the rest up now.

MERCY. Dolly! Dolly lass, what's keepin' ye?

(Enter DOLLY DUTTON, *niece to* DUNSTAN *and* MERCY KIRKE, *employed as maid of all work at Blackburn Mill. She is in her middle to late twenties, dressed in servant clothing. Her speech is that of an uneducated country girl, without the heavy accent of* MERCY *and* DUNSTAN.*)*

DOLLY *(entering with bundles)*. Here I am, Aunt Mercy.

MERCY *(rising)*. Has thee got the homespun, lass?

DOLLY. Aye, here 'tis, bundled and ready to go.

MERCY. That's a good child. Here, tie it up wi' the rest o' these.

DOLLY *(tying bundles)*. La, Aunt Mercy! Is Uncle Kirke going to take all these to market wi' him?

MERCY. Aye, girl—times be hard, and money must be had for Hazel's wedding day.

DOLLY. Hazel's wedding day?

MERCY. Aye, child, that'll be soon now. Her father has decided that Hazel must marry Squire Rodney within three months.

DOLLY. Oh! How I hate that Squire Rodney!

MERCY. Hate him? What for, pray?

DOLLY. For stealing our Hazel away from her happiness.

MERCY. What dost mean, girl?

DOLLY. You're going to make Hazel marry Squire Rodney for gratitude, but it won't do, Aunt Mercy. Gratitude is not the stuff to make a happy marriage of. Can't Uncle pay off the money and let Hazel decide for herself?

MERCY. That he can't—for it takes all he can make to keep the mill a-goin'. Besides, Squire Rodney won't hear of it. He's bound Hazel will keep her promise and be his wife.

DOLLY. But what does Hazel say?

MERCY. She's not mentioned it for weeks. But she's been reared to honor her parents, and I know she'll never go against a promise made to her father. Hazel knows his iron will and harsh ways.

DOLLY. As who doesn't since he drove John—his own brother—from the mill, with a curse on his lips and anger in his heart, simply because he wouldn't be a miller all his life, as Dunstan thought he should.

MERCY. Peace, lass, peace!

DOLLY. La, Aunt Mercy! Thee'd say peace to the wicked one himself, if he were here.

MERCY. I think he be here indeed, Dolly, in thy temper.

DOLLY. Temper! Well, who has a better right to a temper? My mother was thy husband's sister, and all the world knows that Dunstan Kirke has the worst temper in all Lancashire!

DUNSTAN *(offstage, in a rage)*. Coom! Coom! Off wi' ye—don't lollop around here all day! Hoorry to market, and don't loaf, for I'll be after ye wi' the young colt, as fast as ever I can.

DOLLY. Listen to Uncle Kirke, raging like a maddened bull.

MET *(enters, running across stage, frightened)*. Hi! Look out, he's comin'! *(Exit D.R.)*

(DUNSTAN KIRKE enters excitedly. He is a' middle-aged, hard-working miller who has worked outdoors in all kinds of weather all his life.)

DUNSTAN. Drat em! Drat 'em! I say! They're enough to make a devil o' a saint, so they are!

MERCY. There, there, dear heart, *(She crosses to him.)* Have patience, patience.

DUNSTAN. Patience! I am patient—patient as an angel. Confound 'em. It's taken me all day to get 'em off.

(HAZEL KIRKE is heard singing outside. As he listens, DUNSTAN's anger passes away, and he sinks into a chair).

Ah! that does me good! That does me good! My Hazel's a lass, bless her, to gladden a feyther's heart—as modest as a girl should be, and as accomplished as any lady i' the land.

(Enter SQUIRE AARON RODNEY, a country gentleman in his late forties, well-dressed.)

MERCY. Yes, she's well eddicated, now.

DUNSTAN. Thanks to Squire Rodney, God bless him. T'was he got her the larnin'.

DOLLY. And he'll be well paid for it, too, when she's his wife.

DUNSTAN. Weel, that'll soon be now— that'll soon be now.

(MERCY and DOLLY exit into house D.R.)

RODNEY *(advancing)*. I'm not so sure of that.

DUNSTAN. Ah! Maister Rodney, here at last! An' what's that ye're not so sure on?

RODNEY. That Hazel will ever be my wife.

DUNSTAN. Not be thy wife! Why, man, what's coom 'o thee, to say so strange a word? Didn't ye save me from ruin, and the whole mill from changin' hands, four year ago, and didn't Hazel promise then to be your wife, and didn't ye send her off to school, that she might learn to be the lady o' Rodney Hall?

RODNEY. True, Dunstan, but she was only fourteen then. There's many a slip 'twixt the cup and the lip, ye know.

DUNSTAN. Why! whatever do ye mean, man?

RODNEY. Why, I mean accidents may happen, and a young girl's heart may change.

DUNSTAN. Be careful what ye're sayin'! My Hazel—

RODNEY. Since you saved young Carringford from drowning, and brought him here, I've seen a change in Hazel. You don't see with my eyes, Dunstan—you don't see what I see.

DUNSTAN. And what dost see, sir?

RODNEY. I see an idle, handsome man lying ill and helpless. I see a lovely girl waiting upon him—nursing him. I see him looking at her, talking to her, touching her, and I know well what this must come to soon.

DUNSTAN. Maister Rodney, there is a holy book, that my bairn reads to us every day. Dost think that she can ever forget that that book commands us to keep our faith?

RODNEY. Ah, yes, Dunstan, but I warn you—the man bears watching. I've been a man of my word, sir, and I shall expect you to keep yours. You will remember that four years ago when you were on the brink of ruin, I did not at first take kindly to loaning the money.

DUNSTAN. I never did understand what made ye change yer mind.

RODNEY. Only the dictates of a kind heart, Dunstan. No one else would have loaned you money on a crumbling mill and the promise of a young girl's hand. And now that I've expended so much on the girl's education, I mean that she shall keep her promise.

DUNSTAN. That she will! A promise be a promise! If my child were to break her word, I'd drive her out as I would a scorpion on my hearth. Everybody knows the metal I'm made on. What I say, I'll do! And I tell thee now, Aaron Rodney, that this day three months, Hazel Kirke shall be thy wife!

RODNEY. Three months is too long—with young Carringford under your roof; you cannot know what turn events may take. I insist that the marriage shall take place within the week.

DUNSTAN. Why, man! Within the week!

HAZEL (offstage). Thanks—I've found them—I'll go myself.

RODNEY. Hush—that's her voice. We'll speak of this later.

(Enter HAZEL KIRKE, daughter of DUNSTAN and MERCY KIRKE. She is a beautiful young girl, well-dressed, and shows the effect of having been educated away from Blackburn Mill. Her clothes are quiet and tasteful, and her speech has no trace of her parents' accents.)

HAZEL (entering). Here, father, are some letters I want you to post. You won't forget?

DUNSTAN. Nothing that thee can ask, lass—not while thy face shines as bright wi' innocence as it does now! But look, child, there's Maister Rodney, child.

HAZEL. Good morning, Mr. Rodney.

DUNSTAN. Nay, lass, don't mind me. Give him your hand to kiss and a good hearty, honest girl's curtsey.

HAZEL (laughing). That's something I've never refused him yet.

(She does so. RODNEY attempts to embrace her, but HAZEL breaks away.)

Now, here, father, is the list of things for you to get.

DUNSTAN (gathering up bundles on table). A'reet, girl.

HAZEL. And here are my letters. Be sure you don't forget to post them.

DUNSTAN. No, girl, I shan't forget anything. I am not the forgettin' kind. (Starts to go; sees RODNEY and returns to HAZEL.) Ah! But I'm forgettin' one thing now, to ask after Maister Carringford. How is he this mornin', lass?

HAZEL. Better, I think.

DUNSTAN. Ah! He better be. He's been here more nor a month. He's a long time getting well.

HAZEL. But think how horribly he was hurt!

DUNSTAN. Aye, but I've seen older bones sooner mended. It's time he were well and off to his work; this is no place for idle hands. Give him a hint, girl—and here, my darling—gi' me a partin' kiss. God be wi' ye, child, and keep ye always the blessin' that ye are. Coom, Squire, see me to my colt.

(Exits with RODNEY.*)*

HAZEL. Ah! thank heaven he cannot see the wickedness in my wretched, wretched heart.

JOE *(offstage)*. Get out of this!

MET *(offstage)*. Hi! Hold on! Take that!

(Crash is heard.)

HAZEL *(starting)*. What's that?

MET *(enters running)*. Save me! Save me!

HAZEL. And now what have you done?

MET. Not a thing, Miss Hazel; I was only a-standin' blowin' my pipe.

HAZEL. But I've told you to stay out of Joe's way—he has no patience with your foolishness. Now, come with me—

MET. Are ye goin' to Mr. Carringford?

HAZEL. Why do you ask that?

MET. Because if you are, I won't go. I—hate him!

HAZEL. Hate him? What for?

MET. Because you love him so.

HAZEL *(severely)*. How dare you say that!

MET. Because it's true.

HAZEL *(with mock severity, extending her hand)*. Met, come with me this instant.

MET. Where?

HAZEL. To pick some flowers.

MET. Oh! Then I'll go, mistress—then I'll go.

*(*HAZEL *and* MET *exit.)*

RODNEY *(entering)*. There she goes—the fairest lass to ever stroll the moors, and within the week she'll be mine! Her beauty would be prize enough, but the secret I've carried for four long years makes me heir to even more. Who would have dreamed that Dunstan's worthless brother—John—whom he drove out so many years ago, could have amassed so impressive a fortune in diamonds? And to think I nearly turned it down, the richest opportunity of my life! When Dunstan came to me four years ago, begging to be saved from ruin *(Taking letter from pocket inside coat.)*, I laughed at him—and then this letter came. *(Reads.)* "Squire Aaron Rodney, Rodney Hall, Lancashire. My dear Sir, We have to hand the last will and testament of John Richard Kirke, brother of Dunstan Kirke, with whom I believe you are acquainted. It seems that because of an old family quarrel, John Kirke does not want his brother to know that before his untimely death in Africa, he had amassed a considerable fortune which, by his will, he leaves to his niece, Hazel Kirke. The estate is to be left with this firm, in trust for her, until she is of age. However, from the estate, funds have been provided for her education, with the further provision that the estate be placed in her hands only if she leaves her father's mill. If you will come to London, we believe it can be arranged for you to carry out his wishes regarding her education. Trusting you will hold this matter in strictest confidence—." And so, I went to Dunstan with my generous offer, asking no security save the opportunity to educate his lovely daughter. That Dunstan would discover all has oft caused fear to grip my heart; but his iron will doth blind him to the cunning of my ways. And now with Dunstan's promise to hasten Hazel's wedding day, the time is near when both her beauty and her fortune will be mine. One threat remains: Young Carringford! I must arrange that inquiries be made to crush his fondest wish!—But soft, someone comes. *(Exit.)*

(Enter DOLLY, *followed by* BARNEY O'FLYNN, LORD TRAVERS' *valet. His dress is rather formal, his Irish accent heavy.)*

DOLLY. Here is the house and here is the mill you're asking after.

BARNEY. Thankee! Thankee! So there's the mill-dam, where my master was drowned about six weeks since.

DOLLY. And now, who are you, and who did you want to see?

BARNEY. I'm Barney O'Flynn, Miss—the lackey of my lord.

DOLLY. And who's he?

BARNEY. One of your lodgers, I believe.

DOLLY. A lord lodging here? Ye're wrong—man—this is no place for lords.

BARNEY. True enough, darlin', true enough, but still my lord is here.

DOLLY. Will you give me the lie in my own house?

BARNEY. Hould now! Hould! Sure, here's his own direction in my own hand this minute: Lord Travers, at Dunstan Kirke's mill—Blackburn, Lancashire. Isn't this Lancashire?

DOLLY. Yes.

BARNEY. And isn't this Blackburn and the mill o' Dunstan Kirke?

DOLLY. Yes.

BARNEY. Very well, then, Lord Travers is here, just as sure as I'm Barney O'Flynn, and there's the proof of it—a letter calling Master Arthur home to onst.

DOLLY. Arthur, Arthur Carringford?

BARNEY. Yes, of course he's Lord Travers, and my master.

DOLLY. Mr. Carringford a lord!

BARNEY. Of course he's a lord—and I've been down from London to take him home in a howl of a hurry, too. Where is he?

DOLLY. There in the house.

BARNEY. Oh, he is, is he? Now ain't you ashamed of yourself, and you were going to drive me out! "Will ye give me the lie in my own house?" Never mind, darlin', I forgive ye, I forgive —

DOLLY. Get out of here, you fool! *(She chases* BARNEY *off left with a broom.)* Mr. Carringford a lord! And in love with Hazel, too—aye, I know he is—I can see it in his face every time he looks at her. Ah! If poor Hazel were only free, she might be Lady Travers, rich and grand! He has her heart already, aye, and except for Mr. Rodney, he'd have her hand as well. Ah! If I were Hazel, I know what I'd do. *(During speech* DOLLY *has been sorting vegetables from a basket. She holds a carrot through much of the next scene.)* I'd marry the man I loved in spite of all the world. *(She sits.)*

(Enter PITTACUS GREEN, *behind the low stone wall U.R. A slight man, well-dressed as a country gentleman. He doffs his plaid wool hat as he appears.)*

GREEN. Stand where you are! You are the sweetest picture of surprise, that ever yet has blessed my eyes! Oh, 'tis true, and on my soul I swear it! *(He vaults the low stone wall.)* Will you permit me?

DOLLY *(standing)*. Permit you what?

GREEN *(coming to her)*. To change the situation—thus. Ha! Ha!

DOLLY *(backing up)*. Who are you, sir?

GREEN. A hunter of heroes.

DOLLY. What brings you here?

GREEN. A tyrant called Curiosity.

DOLLY. La, the man is mad!

GREEN. No, I grieve to say I am not. I wish I were—madmen are monsters, everything monstrous is fascinating, but I, alas, am not a fascinating man, am I?

DOLLY. La, man, I don't know what ye are.

GREEN. You may not believe it, but I once was born—a baby too! Oh, I tell you, funny things have happened to me. At the early age of one minute, I howled to see the world. Luckily, my father made a handsome fortune in lemonade, by aid of which ade, I'm glad to say, I am enabled now today to see the world and have my way! That way, remark, is this: I go where I please, see what I please, say what I please, and please where I can, do you understand?

DOLLY. No, not a single word you say.

GREEN *(seating himself)*. That's just what I supposed. Then I will be plain with you. I will be plain. A monster or a hero, I adore; ordinary mortals I detest; they are too much like Pittacus Green.

DOLLY. And who is Pittacus Green?

GREEN. The humble and devoted slave now gazing into those lovely eyes. *(He crosses to her, gazing into her eyes.)* Will you permit me to relieve you of that ponderous vegetable that cumbers those lovely hands? *(He takes the carrot from her, puts it down with other vegetables.)*

DOLLY. And so you are Pittacus Green?

GREEN. That is my distinguished name, Pit-ta-cus Green, or, as I'm called for short, Pitty Green. You may not believe it, but they say I'm cracked.

DOLLY. I knew it.

GREEN. Don't be alarmed. It's lovely to be cracked!

DOLLY. Lovely to be cracked!

GREEN. Of course, convince men that you are cracked, and they will let you do the oddest things. They'll smile instead of frown, and to gain a smile from lips like yours, I'd pay any price. Do you understand me now?

DOLLY. I think I do, and I like you, too, and here's Dolly Dutton's hand to prove it.

GREEN. You may not believe it, but you're an angel! Will you permit me? *(Takes her hand.)*

DOLLY. Anything that's honest.

(He kisses her hand.)

GREEN. 'Tis honest. Fair exchange is no robbery.

DOLLY *(sits)*. Now tell me truly—what is it that brings you here?

GREEN. As I said before, a monster or a hero I adore.

DOLLY. And do you expect to find a monster here?

GREEN. Yes, one in particular, one Dunstan Kirke, the miller of Blackburn Mill. He is the monster I mean—the rarest monster ever seen. A monster of goodness, who, during the last ten years, has saved from death by drowning at least forty souls, with their bodies attached.

DOLLY *(rises and crosses D.L.)*. And so, you are here to see my surly old uncle, who saves other folks, perhaps while he destroys his own daughter!

GREEN. Destroys his own daughter? Superb! Does he do it often? I mean, is he taken so frequently? Do sit down, make yourself at home; I do.

(DOLLY sits.)

Tell me all about it. *(He draws up a stool and sits beside her.)*

DOLLY. You've heard of the many he's saved; have you heard of the one he's sold?

GREEN *(rises, leans toward her)*. No, someone sold? Delightful! Who was it?

DOLLY. The pride o' this family, sir, my cousin, Hazel Kirke, she's the one that's sold.

GREEN. Indeed, poor thing, I sympathize; I've sold myself. Who sold her?

DOLLY. Her own feyther, Dunstan Kirke, your hero!

GREEN. Dear me! Why did he do it?

DOLLY. Because he loves his old mill more than anything else in the world. Four years ago, the bank that held my uncle's savings broke, and the old man was about to lose the mill, when Aaron Rodney loaned him the money without interest or security.

GREEN. He was a jolly old idiot! What was his little game?

DOLLY. "Sir," said the Squire, "You have a daughter, whom I admire; give me leave to send her off to school, have her taught, and then become my wife and the lady of Rodney Hall."

GREEN. Ah-ha! I smell a rat! Rodney goes to her, makes love to her, fills her mind with gaudy pictures, chromes and thromes, tells her of the good his wealth will do, and so she, a thoughtless child, makes a rash promise to please her father—which promise is sure to play the dev-Mephistopheles with them both.

DOLLY. Why, man, how did you know that?

GREEN. Quite simply, I guessed it.

DOLLY. Well, then, ye're not so much of a fool as I took ye for.

GREEN. Bless you for those kind words. Tell me what became of your cousin.

DOLLY. Four years ago she was sent to school; six months ago she returned.

GREEN. She is awfully fond of old Rod, of course?

DOLLY. She's proud and silent, sir, but I, who love her, read her heart. I know that she could not love Aaron Rodney.

GREEN. Egad! The situation inspires me! What would you say if I were to help you clear your cousin Hazel of her bargain?

DOLLY. I'd say ye were the best man that ever crossed the threshold of Blackburn Mill.

GREEN. That being the case—what would you give to have it done?

DOLLY. Anything I've got.

GREEN. Even your heart?

DOLLY. La, man! I haven't got any.

GREEN. Haven't you? Well, then would you give this fashionable substitute? *(He indicates carrot.)*

DOLLY. Oh, yes, if ye'd care to take it.

GREEN. Hmm! It's a little moldy, mildew-y, miller-y—the soil of honest labor, I mean. Yes, this is romance, and I'm the Roman. I'll be your best man—I'll outwit old Rod or die.

DOLLY. But how, man, how?

GREEN. You may not believe it, but once I had a mother; funny things have happened to me. That mother, she never could wind a yarn without making a snarl, and I never could undo the snarl without telling a yarn.

DOLLY. What of that?

GREEN. I have great faith in the power of a yarn to undo a snarl. Now there's a snarl in this family; give me leave to tell yarns enough, and I'll guarantee to undo the snarl. Why, bless me, it's perfectly delightful! There's the stern father, Dunstan Kirke; the heavy villain, old Rod; the pretty victim, Hazel Kirke; the scheming cousin, that's you; the good-natured, idiotic busybody, that's me; and—

DOLLY. Why do you stop?

GREEN. Confound it, there's something lacking! We'll imagine here's our Andromeda chained to a rock, about to be devoured by a dragon, a real dragon—wanted: the hero, Perseus, to deliver her. Where shall we get a hero? I have it—we'll advertise! Hello! How's this? Who's that?

DOLLY. Only one of my uncle's patients.

GREEN. Who is he?

DOLLY. Here he comes—find out for yourself.

GREEN. Fate, I thank thee! The conquering hero comes!

(Enter ARTHUR CARRINGFORD, *a young nobleman, Lord Travers. He is handsome and his speech and manner reveal his class and education. He is dressed in rough country clothing that has been loaned to him since his accident at the mill.)*

ARTHUR. Have you seen my dog? Ah, Miss Dolly!

DOLLY. She went off with Met a while ago. Shall I find her for you?

ARTHUR. You're very kind. If it isn't too much trouble, I should be glad of a little of Miss Hazel's company, if she's at leisure. You know I must soon leave this dear place.

DOLLY. I'll try and find her, sir.

GREEN. Ye great god of war.

ARTHUR. Ha—what idiot is this?

GREEN. It is! It is! By the bolts of Jove, it is!

ARTHUR. Indeed! Is it—what is?

GREEN. You is—either I'm a cow, or this is Lord Travers.

ARTHUR. Who is Lord Travers? You—

GREEN. You is—am—are. Look at me sharp. Don't you remember P.G.? Have you forgotten our tiger hunt in India? Ah, there was a monster worth meeting! He met you and treed you, too. Can't you recall your old comrade of the jungle, Pittacus—the mouse that freed you, the lion? Why, it was the proudest shot of my life!

ARTHUR. On my life—is it possible—you here?

GREEN. Of course I am! And *(They shake hands.)* bless my soul, how glad I am to see you.

ARTHUR. Hold on—the arm you are torturing is only half mended.

GREEN. Gracious! What do you mean?

ARTHUR. That this is a broken arm but slightly convalescent.

GREEN. A broken arm, forgive me! Travers, I'm a brute! Take that indigestible vegetable and crack my skull.

ARTHUR. Thanks, dear boy, it's cracked enough already.

GREEN. Precisely; I see your vengeance is complete.

ARTHUR. Now tell me how you found me out?

GREEN. By accident—the usual way. How did you get here?

ARTHUR. Came to Lancashire to escape the tiresome nonsense of town—went shooting with my dog—attempted to cross the stream by a tree that lay over it, just above the dam—there.

GREEN. Then what?

ARTHUR. Slipped like a fool, fell, broke my arm in falling and sank unconscious into the water.

GREEN. Merciful powers!

ARTHUR. My dog sprang in and held me above the surface. Kirke, the miller, caught sight of us and jumped in, pulled me out and lodged me here, where I've had the best of care for six weeks.

GREEN. Great fortune! I see it all. It's the saved and the sold, side by side, beneath the same roof; she is the sold and you are now the saved, two hearts with but a single stock. Travers, my dear boy, you may not believe it, but there's more than accident in this arrangement.

ARTHUR. Undoubtedly, but your exclamations are somewhat obscure.

GREEN. Look here, old man, let's get to business. Time flies. I helped you when you were in a pickle; now you must help me.

ARTHUR. With pleasure! How can I do it?

GREEN. By falling desperately in love.

ARTHUR. Oh, falling in love! Why, that's your business; you know you are always falling in love.

GREEN. And why not? As the poet says, come live with me and be my love. I love to live and I live to love.

ARTHUR. Eccentric dog! You always manage to make logic and delight agree.

GREEN. Oh, Travers, I've met my fate at last!

ARTHUR. Nonsense, you are always meeting your fate—who is she this time?

GREEN. Dolly Dutton, the miller's niece.

ARTHUR. You'll find her rather a lively fate, I fancy.

GREEN. Precisely! I know I shall, that's the way I like 'em. She's a perfect monster.

ARTHUR. Monster?

GREEN. Yes, a monster of beauty and goodness—but come—will you do me a favor and fall in love?

ARTHUR. Certainly. I find there's nothing easier than to fall; I've tried one element, I've no fear to try another. With whom must I fall in love?

GREEN. An angel in a fix; Hazel Kirke, the miller's daughter.

ARTHUR. Stop, sir, I shall not tolerate nonsense that touches her good name. Understand this at once.

GREEN. Capital! I'm more than satisfied! I'm ecstatic. You're in love with her already.

ARTHUR. Sir! Green, Miss Kirke is coming. I'm known here simply as Arthur Carringford, you must not betray my title; it would only raise a barrier between me and the golden hearts to whom I owe so much.

GREEN. Travers, I honor your sentiments, and will respect your wishes.

DOLLY *(entering)*. Here she is, Maister Carringford.

(Enter HAZEL and MET.)

HAZEL. Now, Met, go to Mother Weedbury's cottage and carry some wood for the poor thing and stop there till I come. Tell her I will be there to help her with the children in the morning.

MET. All right, Miss, I'll go; but mind it's for you and not for the old woman. *(Exits.)*

HAZEL. Good morning, Mr. Carringford.

ARTHUR. Miss Hazel, I'm glad to have a glimpse of you at last.

GREEN. Have mercy! Why don't you present me to the lady?

ARTHUR. Miss Kirke, permit me to present a very dear old friend, Mr. Pittacus Green.

HAZEL. He's doubly welcome, as your friend, and for his own sake.

GREEN. Ah! Miss Kirke *(Kisses her hand.)*, I'm a very old-fashioned young fool. You will permit me? I am your slave. Pittacus, there's no use, you're an assassin from this hour; the one dear purpose of your life is to get Squire Rodney cremated without delay.

HAZEL *(offers flowers)*. Let me share my treasures. There—what do you say to that?

GREEN. I say nothing, nothing! I am dumb with delight, decidedly, Old Rod is a doomed man.

HAZEL. Will you accept a flower?

ARTHUR. Thanks. Miss Hazel, I know I sent for you, but if you will permit me, I'd like to retire to my room with my friend Mr. Green for a talk of old times.

HAZEL. Of course. Sorry to lose you.

*(*ARTHUR *exits U.L.)*

GREEN. My dear Miss Kirke, you may not believe it, but by the justice of Jove, we'll meet again.

*(*HAZEL *exits U.L.* GREEN *begins to hum snatch of a song.)*

DOLLY. Stop! Stop! Look here, you've promised to help me free my cousin Hazel from her bargain with the Squire. When are you going to begin?

GREEN. Dear Dolly Dutton: I've just begun, and you must help. First, you must see her mother and tell her you know that Rodney is not the man Hazel loves.

DOLLY. I'd never dare do that!

GREEN. What? You can't desert me now—I'm forming plans and you must help. So, courage, speak, and your cousin will be blessed! Here her Aunt comes, I'll leave her to the tender mercies of your tongue. Madam, will you permit me? In the words of the immortal bard of Avon, I humbly take my leaf. Madam, if all the world were right, you and I would never be in the wrong!

(Exit U.L. MERCY *enters from house.)*

MERCY. Dolly, who be that?

DOLLY. A man named Pitty Green.

MERCY. Pitty Green. An odd name, and he seems a bit off *(Taps her head.)* here!

DOLLY. That's all right, Aunt, so long as he is sound here. *(Hand to her heart.)*

MERCY. Aye, that's true, Dolly, that's true.

DOLLY. Aunt Mercy—

MERCY. Well, Dolly?

DOLLY. Did ye mark the look in Hazel's face this morning, after her father told her Mr. Carringford had been here long enough?

MERCY. What sort o' look, girl?

DOLLY. A pale, suffering, frightened look. Aunt, she's in love with Mr. Carringford, as sure as I'm a living woman.

MERCY *(with a start)*. My heart, child! Does thee mean what thee says? *(Stands.)*

DOLLY. Indeed I do.

(Enter HAZEL*.)*

HAZEL. Mother dear, be sure to let me know when father has finished his supper and settled his accounts. You won't forget?

MERCY. Where are thee going, child?

HAZEL. I'm going to Mother Weedbury's cottage to fetch Met home.

MERCY. Thee can wait a bit. I've a word to say to thee. Dolly, thee'll find work in the house. Leave us.

DOLLY. All right, aunt. *(Exit D.R.)*

MERCY. Hazel, child, come here and kneel at my feet as thee did when a little one, and I taught thee to pray. My child, many in this world may say they love thee, but none'll ever do it as I do. Thee may have friends and lovers, too, but thee can never have but one mother. Well, child, can't thee trust her?

HAZEL. Trust her? Have I ever distrusted her?

MERCY. Aye, thee's distrustin' her now. There's that in thy heart she ought to know.

HAZEL. Why, mother, what do you mean?

MERCY. Oh, thee knows well eno' what I mean. I've been foolish, child, and blind. I forgot the danger o' youthful blood, and I felt too sure o' thy promise to be Aaron Rodney's wife. But my eyes are open now. I've discovered thy secret, girl. And I must speak to thee.

HAZEL. Oh, mother—spare me—it is too late! It is too late!

MERCY. Too late! What dost mean, child? Speak! Lift up thy head and look me in the face.

HAZEL. Mother!

MERCY. Ah! It's a'reet, ye can look me i' the eye still, like an honest girl. But oh, I see it all now. That Maister Carringford be a bad man—a bad man.

HAZEL. Mother!

MERCY. There's no use, Hazel—I know all thee'll say for him! But thy feyther saved his life and cherished him in his house, and this is his gratitude, to make love to thee—the plighted wife o' another man.

HAZEL. No, mother, you wrong him. He has never spoken a word of love to me in his life.

MERCY. An' has thee been won then wi'out wooing?

HAZEL. Oh,how can I tell? All that I know is that day by day his voice grows sweeter, his words wiser. I did not realize how empty my life would be without him till now the time has come for him to go. It seems as if the shadow of death were upon my heart—it has grown so dull and heavy!

MERCY. Does thee say that he has never told thee that he loves thee?

HAZEL. Never! And yet I know he does. When my back is turned, I can feel his eyes upon me—I saw them once by accident in the glass. I knew all then, for I saw in them my own misery, my own love. *(She goes to* MERCY's *arms.)*

MERCY. My poor child! But we must do right, if it kills us. There's but one remedy for this, the short and sharp one. *(She starts to go.)*

HAZEL. Where are you going, Mother?

MERCY. He must leave this house at once. *(Crosses D.R. to go.)*

HAZEL *(stops her).* No, it is not for you to send him away; that is my duty. It will be less of an insult to him and less agony to me.

MERCY. Thou hast not the strength to do it.

HAZEL. I will find it. Send him here to me, and I promise you I will tell him we must part at once.

MERCY *(speaks as she goes).* Aye, it's better so. Perhaps thee'll fret less if thee send him away. Thee shall have thy way, Hazel child.

*(*HAZEL *comes to her and she kisses her.)*

Courage, lass, be strong i' the battle today, and thou'lt be rich i' the triumph tomorrow. *(She exits.)*

HAZEL. What am I going to do? Drive away the happiness that heaven sends me? Insult the man I honor most—and all for what? To keep the rash promise of a silly, thoughtless girl? *(She sits.)* Oh, I must not think of it, or I shall rebel.

(Enter ARTHUR*)*

ARTHUR. Why, Hazel, what's the matter?

(She rises coldly.)

Pardon me, Miss Kirke, you wished to speak to me?

HAZEL. Mr. Carringford, I have sent for you to say that which may sound strangely coming from me—but you must leave this place at once.

ARTHUR. Leave? May I know why?

HAZEL. No. Not from my lips.

ARTHUR. Do you wish me to go?

HAZEL. Yes, yes, go—and quickly!

ARTHUR. You are right—I will go.

(Unseen by them, RODNEY *enters U.L.)*

(Extends his hand to her.) Bid me farewell.

(She turns away, holding her hand out toward him. He kisses it tenderly. She falls sobbing in chair.)

You must have mercy upon me and let me speak.

HAZEL. No. I beseech you, leave me—in kindness, leave me without a word.

(He turns to go; RODNEY *steps forward.)*

RODNEY. Stay, Mr. Carringford, one word with you. I know all; I have seen how you have come into this house and made light with the affections of Miss Kirke.

(HAZEL *draws back.*)

I see how you have tried to win her from me—but you know she is my plighted wife.

HAZEL. You need say no more, Mr. Rodney—Mr. Carringford is leaving.

RODNEY. But I would say more. Mr. Carringford, I know who you are. I have taken the precaution of writing to your mother—you know the pride of your race, sir. Your mother would never consent to your marriage with this miller's daughter.

HAZEL. I beg you—stay your words—I do not understand their meaning, but Mr. Carringford is leaving at once. I cannot help the past, but I can be brave for the future. I can do my duty and keep my promise.

ARTHUR. No, Hazel! Your promise of the past was clouded in the innocence of childhood. Your duty to the future is to marry the man you love!

RODNEY (*steps toward* HAZEL, *she recoils*). And I—Mr. Carringford— claim to be that man!

ARTHUR (*stepping between them*). What demon would desire the plighted love of a righteous girl knowing full well that time alone and only the bower of true womanhood may bestow such a gift? I tell you, sir, your intentions are dishonorable!

RODNEY. I warn you, Carringford, you tread on treacherous ground. (*Backing off.*) I leave you to your fond farewells. Should you remain when I return, I'll demonstrate what sort of demon you defy! (*Exit.*)

(ARTHUR *starts after him but is stopped by* HAZEL.)

HAZEL. No, Arthur! Let him go. My father must never know the love I promised one man has been given to another. That secret must be kept, though it tear our lives apart! Until you came I never dreamed the sweetness such a love could bring. (HAZEL *goes to him, puts her hands up to his chest and looks in his eyes.*) Your eyes, your voice, your words have brought a singing to my heart! That song will last forever. (*She turns away, dropping head.*) I must not ask for more.

ARTHUR. Ah, Heaven! (*He takes her hand.*) This is the bitterest and sweetest moment of my life!

(*Enter* DUNSTAN *with bundles.* HAZEL *and* ARTHUR *separate.*)

DUNSTAN. Ah, lass, and here's thy bundles.

HAZEL. Father! But how quickly you've returned!

DUNSTAN. Aye, lass, there was a letter at post, so I hurried home. They said it was for me. Here, lass, read it for me. Let me hear what it says.

(*He hands her the letter; she opens it and starts.*)

Well, lass, and what says the letter?

(HAZEL *becomes faint. He assists her to a chair.*)

My heart, child, what be the matter? There, sit down, sit down;

what's the trouble? Is it bad news? Out with it. Who's it from? Let's hear.

HAZEL. It is signed "Emily Carringford."

(ARTHUR *starts.*)

DUNSTAN. What ha' she got to say to me? Read it, lass; what does she say?

HAZEL (*aside*). There's no use. I shall be forced to read it. "Dunstan Kirke, Esq., Dear Sir, I have been startled by learning of my son's presence in your home, deeply pained by hearing of his conduct with your child—"

DUNSTAN. Eh? What be that? What be that?

HAZEL. "I have besought him to return to me instantly. If he refuses, I call on you to add the force of your commands to my prayers."

DUNSTAN. Aye, aye, it's gettin' clearer, it's gettin' clearer. Go on child, what more does she say?

HAZEL. "I cannot describe my indignation at the thought of my son's love for—"(*She breaks down.*)

DUNSTAN. That's enough! Stop there, girl—ya need read no more! Mr. Carringford, I'd been warned and thought y' more of a man than ye are! I've only one child in all the world, and God knows I love her, better than my life. Well, sir, I'd rather bury her with my own hands than have her faithless to her word. Now, ye know she's the plighted wife o' Aaron Rodney. Well, then, are ye a serpent I've cherished in my breast to bite me and mine? Have ye dared to think o' making love to Hazel Kirke?

ARTHUR. Fate threw me helpless at her feet. 'Twas these hands (*Holding her hands.*) nursed me back to life. Well, sir, I confess what I could not wish to help—I learned to love her!

DUNSTAN. Hazel, thee hears what he says, and thee knows the duty o' an honest girl. Bid him be gone at once!

HAZEL. No, Father, I cannot.

DUNSTAN. What's that thee says?

HAZEL. If he must go, I should go, for I too am guilty.

DUNSTAN. What! My child avows dishonor?

HAZEL. Father—Father, hear me!

DUNSTAN. Hear thee! No, no! (*Advancing toward her.*) I've heard too much already. I could take thy shameless heart out.

(HAZEL *with a cry of fear, draws back into* ARTHUR's *arms.*)

ARTHUR (*shielding her*). Stand back, sir, stand back!

DUNSTAN. What! In his arms! Before my very eyes? Out upon thee, thou foul disgrace! Hear thy father's curse!

(*Enter* MERCY *and rushes to him, pleading,* DOLLY *follows her and stands watching.*)

MERCY. No, no, she is thy child, thine only child!

DUNSTAN (*throws her off*). Begone! Thou misbegotten bairn, begone! I cast thee out adrift, adrift forever from they feyther's love, and may my eyes no more behold thee!

HAZEL. Mother! Mother!

(MERCY *starts toward* HAZEL. DUNSTAN *comes between them.*)

DUNSTAN. Stand back! She is lost to thee forever!

TABLEAU. HAZEL *in* ARTHUR'*s arms, arms outstretched toward* MERCY *and* DUNSTAN; MERCY *silently pleading with* DUNSTAN; DOLLY *dropping her head in dejection.*)

CURTAIN

Arthur. "May all our troubles end like this—in smoke and a kiss." (In Act Two—with Cynthia Montilla as Hazel and William Halliday as Arthur.)

ACT TWO

SCENE: *Interior of* LORD TRAVERS' *villa at Fairy Grove; a room bright with sunlight. On a table L. are cigarettes and matches, also a bell; water and glass are on a stand R. At rise of curtain,* AARON RODNEY *opens the door quietly and peers about. Seeing no one, he steps inside. Outside,* MET *can be heard blowing her pipe.*

RODNEY. Ha, no one about! So this is the nest where Carringford has hidden her all these months from the shame of a pretended marriage too hideous to serve the fine and noble manners of his titled race! I have had the devil's own time finding her myself while I kept the lawyers from locating her to give her the estate. Fortunately, the fools believed me when I told them that she had had a serious illness, was travelling on the continent, and could not be reached, but I surely cannot hold them off much longer. Time is of the essence and I must act with haste! Now—if only Carringford is not about, I shall bring his mother, Lady Travers, here to tell Hazel that this marriage to her son was a fraud. That done and Hazel in tears—I shall offer my forgiveness, agree to marry her in spite of her ah—sin, and she cannot fail, in gratitude, to allow me free rein with her fortune! Ssst—someone comes. *(Exit.)*

(Enter BARNEY.*)*

BARNEY. There's that worthless girl blowin' the pipe again, instead o' mindin' the kitchen. Why did Mr. Carringford ever let that ninny here!

(Enter MET *carrying flowers.)*

MET. I say, where's the mistress, Barney?

BARNEY. And what would you be wantin' of her now?

MET. Here's some flowers I've been picking for her. Where is she?

BARNEY. Oh, about some'res—cryin', I suppose.

MET. Cryin'—What do you mean?

BARNEY. Well, if you was half as witted as ye seem, ye'd know that for the past three days, she's been mighty put out about somethin'.

MET. What could be the matter with her?

BARNEY. Lonesome, I suppose. She goes nowheres, sees nobody, and for more'n a week Lord Travers has been gone. There's something wrong between 'em, Met. Do you know what it be?

MET. How should I know?

BARNEY. Well, you know the missus before she came here—she brought you here.

MET. No, she didn't bring me here; I followed her, and I'd follow her to the other end of the earth if she'd let me. She's a lady, she is, every inch of her, and she's too good for him!

BARNEY. Too good for my master—watch what ye say, girl!

MET. Well, look at the way he treats her. Why is it he brings no one here to see her. Why is it his mother and none o' his folks don't never come here at all?

BARNEY. How should I know?

MET. Well, ye know more'n you're tellin', to be sure. There she be on the shore of the Park Lake. I'll take her the flowers. *(Plays pipe.)*

BARNEY. Hold on, Met, tell me first—

MET. I'll tell ye nothin', and that's more than ye desarve. *(Exit U.R.)*
(RODNEY enters U.C.)

RODNEY. I say, man, is this place called Fairy Grove?

BARNEY. Yes, sire, that it is.

RODNEY. And is your master at home?

BARNEY. No, sir, that he's not.

RODNEY. And your mistress?

BARNEY. You mean Mrs. Carringford?

RODNEY. Is she called that here?

BARNEY. Indeed she is—for that's her name, sir! Did you wish to see her?

RODNEY. No—no—but I would speak with you. Have you been in service with the Carringford family for long?

BARNEY. Iver since my lord was a boy—and my father before me.

RODNEY. Ah, then, you will understand what a disgrace Lord Travers has brought upon his name.

BARNEY. An' what would ye be meaning?

RODNEY. I mean his—ah—presumed marriage to the common daughter of a miller.

BARNEY. What do you know of it? And by whose leave do you come around askin' questions?

RODNEY. My good man—I am an old friend of the Carringford family and have known Lady Travers for many years. I know that it would break her heart if she knew that her son lives in sin—

BARNEY. In sin, sir? *(Aside.)* How much does he know?

RODNEY. Yes, it has come to my attention that their marriage was falsely performed, and that young Lord Travers practiced the deceit, knowing that the marriage was not legal. Now, I should like to ask a favor of you for which I am willing to pay you well.
*(He takes bills from his pocket and holds them toward BARNEY.
BARNEY reaches; RODNEY withdraws them.)*

BARNEY. Yes?

RODNEY. Yes. I would like you to say, when you are asked, that you were with them when the ceremony was performed. *(Holding the money in front of him carelessly.)*

BARNEY. But I was, sir!

RODNEY. So much the better—I want you to swear that they were married in a Scottish ceremony on the English side of the border.

BARNEY *(aside)*. How could he know? I'd swear no one knew. *(To RODNEY.)* Well, now, I don't know about that.

RODNEY. Come now, if you will do as I say, it will be worth a hundred pounds to you.
(Extends bills. BARNEY grabs them and counts quickly.)

BARNEY. Oh, no, ye don't do that to Barney O'Flynn! There's only fifty here.

RODNEY. I'll pay you the rest when his Lordship has gotten rid of this peasant girl!

BARNEY. Well, then, I'll do it. *(Pockets the money.)* Sure, it's not for the money, you understand, but for the honor of the family I sarve. *(Pats his pocket.)*

RODNEY. Of course, of course. *(Aside.)* They're all alike—the greedy thieves! Now mind you don't say a word until you're asked. I'll be back within the day to see what turn events have taken. *(Exit.)*

BARNEY. Now, who could he be to be so interested in Lord Travers affairs? Ah, well, I've got the fifty pounds, and I'll decide myself who and what I'll tell!

(Enter ARTHUR *D.R., with overcoat over arm.)*

ARTHUR. Well, Barney! *(Tosses overcoat to* BARNEY.*)*

BARNEY. Master, ye frightened me, sure, sir, I'm glad ye're back.

ARTHUR. Where's my wife?

BARNEY. Your wife, sir?

ARTHUR. Certainly, my wife.

BARNEY. Oh, yes, certainly, she's in the garden, I believe.

ARTHUR *(sits at table).* Let her know that I've arrived.

BARNEY. All right, sir. *(Aside.)* He's in one o' his quare moods again. *(Pacing.)* He's gettin' tired of this already. I knew it! I knew it! He'll end it sooner than I thought he would. Ah, there's nothing like a Scottish marriage on the wrong side of the line to save the trouble of divorce and chate the lawyers. *(Exit.)*

ARTHUR *(reads from letter).* "My dear Travers, your mother is in a very dangerous condition. Today she arose for the first time in months, laboring under some strong excitement that is giving her temporary strength. She asks the most searching questions concerning you. She gets more impatient every day for your marriage with 'Lady Maud'." *(Folds letter.)* I had hoped for good news. Ah, will this never end? How long must I conceal my marriage to Hazel? Shall I never be able to show the world the noble woman who is my wife? *(Sinks into reverie.)*

(HAZEL *runs in. Seeing* ARTHUR, *she creeps up behind him and puts her hands over his eyes. He exclaims.)*

HAZEL. Ah, you are back at last, my darling!

ARTHUR. Apparently.

HAZEL. Oh, I'm so glad, so glad! I've been almost dead with loneliness.

ARTHUR. Have you really missed me so much?

HAZEL. More than you will ever know or care, I fear.

ARTHUR. Oh, I love to have you miss me.

HAZEL. Of course you do—you wouldn't love me if you didn't.

ARTHUR. And you're not tired yet of these iron bonds of matrimony?

HAZEL. I call them golden bonds.

ARTHUR. And so they are, and so they are, darling. May they always hold us heart to heart.

HAZEL *(sadly)*. Heigh ho!

ARTHUR. Heigh ho? Well, well, what does this mean?

HAZEL. Oh, only a silly thought. I'm superstitious; too much happiness is dangerous, sometimes, you know, that's all.

ARTHUR *(taking her hand)*. Little woman, do you know I'm not blind—there's something troubles you. What is it?

HAZEL *(imitating him)*. Big man, do you know I'm not blind, and there's something troubles you? What is it?

ARTHUR. Come, come, dear, I'm in earnest.

HAZEL. And so am I, dear. For the last few weeks, whenever you're at home, you've been so silent and moody. Oh, Arthur, can't you trust me with your sorrows as well as your joys? Come, dear, tell me what troubles you.

ARTHUR. Business, that is all. But you, Hazel, you have no such cause for sadness.

HAZEL *(laughing, she rises)*. I sad? Why, I'm the gayest creature in the world.

ARTHUR *(holds her hands)*. You try to be—before me—but when you've supposed me absent, I've seen you in tears. Have I not done all that I could to make you happy?

HAZEL. Oh, indeed you have!

ARTHUR. Then why have I failed?

HAZEL. Failed! You have not failed. You have made me too happy. My happiness startles me sometimes; I so little deserve it. I confess at moments I am haunted.

ARTHUR. Haunted by what, dear?

HAZEL. I hardly know—a vague, uncertain dread. This last year has been so strange, the way we met, our secret marriage in Scotland—

ARTHUR. Yes, but you know why our marriage had to be so secret.

HAZEL. Yes, because your mother had set her heart upon another woman for you.

ARTHUR. My mother has been determined to make me the husband of Maud Wetherby; she has been very ill for years. To have acknowledged my marriage with you would surely have been to kill her. So I was forced to have our marriage take place in the way that offered the least risk of discovery by her.

HAZEL. Oh, my darling, I do hate this hiding! How much longer must it last?

ARTHUR. I have been hoping every day that my mother would have grown strong enough to learn the truth, but I am disappointed; she is no better, I even fear she is growing worse.

HAZEL. Your mother deceived! My father broken-hearted! Oh! It is horrible, I cannot stand it.

ARTHUR. What a fool I've been!

HAZEL. What do you mean?

ARTHUR. I've been stupid enough to fancy that my love—my devotion—might suffice to make you forget—to make you happy.

HAZEL *(going to him)*. And so they do, dear. I was wrong to confess these foolish fears to you. Say you forgive me?

ARTHUR *(embracing her)*. Forgive me that I have not rendered you the open honor that was due you as my wife. *(He turns his head away.)*

HAZEL. How strangely you say that! What can you mean?

ARTHUR. No matter now, dear. *(Affecting gaiety.)* Away with gloomy thoughts! All's well that ends well! Where are my cigarettes—no objection to my smoking, dear?

HAZEL. No, on the contrary, I'll light one for you.

ARTHUR. Thanks, that will be delightful.

(She lights it—draws and coughs.)

HAZEL. There—take the horrid thing.

ARTHUR. Horrid thing! *(Puts his arm around her.)* Why, I declare it's the most delicious cigarette I've ever smoked in all my life. Thanks, little woman, may all our sorrows end like this, in smoke and a kiss.

(He kisses her; she smiles up at him. Meanwhile, PITTACUS GREEN has appeared at the window and observed. He enters C., laden with sporting traps, a sun umbrella over his head. He coughs.)

I declare—at last, it's our dear old Green.

GREEN. Tis true, 'tis Pitty, and pity 'tis, 'tis true. You may not believe it, but all these things are a bore.

HAZEL *(goes to him)*. Talk of matrimonial misery—what is it compared to the awful doom of a bachelor devoted to sport?

GREEN. Oh, I say, don't make sport of a man in mortal agony. Be heroic, come to the rescue, take the umbrageous curio. *(Handing HAZEL his umbrella.)* The idea! Billing and cooing still—a year after marriage, too. It's an outrage on society!

ARTHUR *(having unloaded him)*. So it is, Green! Now, tell us, to what do we owe your sudden advent here?

GREEN *(circles and sits left)*. To the same old lady, Dame Rumor, the despot of my life.

HAZEL. Ah, what monstrous thing has she reported here?

GREEN. Monstrous bliss! The fame of your fishes, the taste of your game, the sound of your kisses is wafted on the breath of rumor to the uttermost end of an envious world. So here am I, with all my senses, wild to see, hear, smell, taste and touch. I'll begin with touch. Give me your fists, ye pair of blissful curiosities! *(Taking them by the hands, he points to her hand.)* Won't you share your monstrosities with me?

HAZEL *(with laughter)*. All we can.

GREEN. All but the kisses, I suppose.

HAZEL *(sitting)*. But what are you going to give us for letting you into our paradise?

GREEN. For you I have some news, and for that mortal I have a sermon.

ARTHUR. Well, let it be a galloping sermon, then. I'll go and order the horses at once. *(Strikes bell on table.)*

GREEN. Capital!

ARTHUR. I'm off. Beware, I have my eye upon you. *(Exit.)*

GREEN. Keep your ear off, that's all we ask.

(Enter BARNEY, R.)

HAZEL. Now for your news.

GREEN. I'm just from Blackburn Mill.

HAZEL. And you have letters for me?

GREEN. No—your father declares that the first who writes you shall leave his house.

HAZEL. Is he still so angry with me then?

GREEN. Angry with you? That's putting it mild. I call him the pig-headedest old heart I ever knew. He won't even let them breathe your name. In fact, there were some men from London at the old mill asking for you; he told them he never had a daughter!

HAZEL. Someone looking for me? Who could that have been—I know no one in London. But how did you learn all this?

GREEN. Dolly told me.

HAZEL. Dolly, is that what you call her?

GREEN. Oh, yes, if a person's name is Dolly, no harm to call her so. Oh, I forgot, you don't know, do you?

HAZEL. Know what?

GREEN. Why, about Dolly—she's going to make a fool of herself.

HAZEL. How?

GREEN. By becoming the better half of P. Green. Pity, isn't it?

HAZEL. Do you mean to say you're going to marry my cousin?

GREEN. Oh, no. She's going to marry me.

HAZEL. Oh, I'm so glad. *(Offers her hand in congratulation.)*

GREEN. You may not believe it, but so am I.

HAZEL *(sitting on couch)*. Tell me all about it.

GREEN. Oh, it was all just like Dolly herself, short and sweet. After you left Lancashire, the doors of the old mill were sternly closed, especially against me. But it didn't matter, you see. I always have an object in life, so suddenly I became interested in dams—mill dams. There was one near the mill; there always is a dam attached to a mill. I used to visit that dam and sketch the dam—the sight of anything dammed was a relief to me. Weeks passed, but the door of the old mill remained closed. Fever ensued; I got dam on the brain and went about muttering dam, dam, all day. However, nothing could dampen the ardor of my disease. At last the crisis approached, Dolly appeared, and took Pitty. Yes, she relieved my delirium and consented to become ma-dam.

HAZEL. You dear, silly old thing. So you're going to become my cousin.

GREEN. Bless me—so I am. I didn't think of that! Now, will you permit me? *(Kisses her hand.)*

*(*ARTHUR *enters.)*

ARTHUR. Hallo! I say!

GREEN. So do I—I say. I not only say, but I do, don't I? I say, cousinship is good. *(He kisses* HAZEL's *hand again.)* A duty I owe to society.

ARTHUR. What does the rascal mean?

HAZEL. Something wonderful.

GREEN. Hush! Quietly; his nerves are weak. Have you ordered the horses?

ARTHUR. Yes, but—

GREEN. But me no buts. Hazel, my dear, go and get ready to drive, and leave this reprobate to the tender mercies of the family high minister, your cousin, Pit.

HAZEL. Oh, very well. Don't forget the sermon. *(Exit.)*

ARTHUR. Now, sir, please explain? *(Slaps* GREEN *on back.)*

GREEN. I explain? Why, sir, I've traveled three hundred miles to make you explain.

ARTHUR. Explain what?

GREEN *(handing* ARTHUR *piece of newspaper).* That, sir.

ARTHUR *(reads).* "Another important engagement in high life announced—that of Lord Travers to Lady Maud Wetherby."

GREEN. Yes, sir; that, sir, is a cutting from the *Morning Post*—a most respectable paper—a very reliable authority.

ARTHUR. Evidently.

GREEN. I don't see anything to laugh at.

ARTHUR. Silly, how can I marry since I am already married?

GREEN. But confound it, sir, you're not married.

ARTHUR. Are you mad?

GREEN. Yes, sir, I am, blind mad—who wouldn't be under the circumstances?

ARTHUR. By Jove—you are insane!

GREEN. Insane? It is you who are insane. Is it nothing to deceive an honest girl into believing she's married when she isn't? Is it nothing to be a smooth, cool, calculating villain, and stand there and look as innocent and serene as an angel?

ARTHUR. My dear boy—of whom are you talking?

GREEN. Oh, this is wicked—wicked—Travers. That's pure malignant cruelty. Haven't I always been a loyal friend?

ARTHUR. Of course you have.

GREEN. Then why couldn't you have trusted me?

ARTHUR. I've never distrusted you.

GREEN. Oh, yes you have; you dealt with me in a beastly manner. You've made me an unconscious accomplice in a piece of business I despise.

ARTHUR. There you go again. Can't you just tell me plainly what in the world you mean?

GREEN. Travers, you're either the most accomplished hypocrite or the biggest fool in the world. If you really don't know—well, I don't know how to begin. You see, I've been sneaking about the old mill lately, and a rumor reached me there that just covered me with goose flesh. It seems old Squire Rodney has been looking into your affairs, and by Jove, he swears you've deceived Hazel!

ARTHUR. Deceived her? How?

GREEN. He said that your marriage to her was a pretence, a farce, a lie!

ARTHUR. And you, my friend, believed him?

GREEN. How could I help it? The whole thing is so circumstantial. He declares that he has positive proof that you went towards Scotland with the pretence of marrying Hazel by Scottish law, but that you cunningly stopped on the border and went through the flimsy Scottish ceremony on English ground.

ARTHUR. An infamous slander!

GREEN. Can you prove that?

ARTHUR. I'll soon convince you. *(He strikes the bell.)*

GREEN. How?

ARTHUR. By the testimony of a witness to my marriage—Barney.

GREEN. Barney! He's the very one Rodney named as your accomplice.

ARTHUR. Accomplice? We shall see—I'll call him.

GREEN. Wait—before you call him—I have more to tell you.

ARTHUR. What more?

GREEN. Dolly told me that there were two men from London calling at the mill to inquire for Hazel, but that Dunstan told them he had no daughter.

ARTHUR. Of course, he would—the ill-tempered old fool!

GREEN. But neither Dolly nor I could figure out who could be looking for Hazel, so when I was last in London, I took it upon myself to make some inquiries.

ARTHUR. And what did you discover?

GREEN. Very little—I was only able to find out that the gentlemen who called are representatives of the law firm of Bates & Bristol. I went to them to discover what I could, but they were very sparing with their information and would tell me nothing. I made up my mind to ask you when I came here, since I knew you would be familiar with her affairs. What do you know of it?

ARTHUR. Not a thing. I can't think why any law firm would be trying to communicate with Hazel.

GREEN. Unless old Rod is still trying to find her—and hopes to locate her through them. It seems they handle a good deal of estate work. Could it be that your wife is coming into a large inheritance?

ARTHUR. Nonsense, you know her family has nothing.

GREEN. Of course, but still—

ARTHUR. Forget it, Green—it is presently much more important that I settle with Barney! If he's been in league with old Rodney to disgrace my wife, he shall answer for it!

GREEN. Hold on! Let me question him. We want to get at the truth, you know, and these chaps easily slip into a lie.

ARTHUR. I don't understand.

GREEN. You will presently.

(Enter BARNEY.*)*

Barney, your master called you because the time has come for us to settle a certain matter, and we wish to be sure that everything is all right, you know.

BARNEY. Faith, sir, I'm at your service.

GREEN. Well, then, my good Barney, tell us frankly, are you quite sure that the town where Lord Travers went through the ceremony of marriage with Miss Kirke was not in Scotland? Well—answer my question.

BARNEY. I will, sir, when my master bids me.

GREEN. Shall he answer my question?

ARTHUR. Certainly, Barney, speak freely.

BARNEY. Well, then, sir, your question be a quare one.

GREEN. In what respect?

BARNEY. Do ye think I'd betray my master?

GREEN. Of course not.

BARNEY. I was brought up in the service of the gentry, sir, all my life. I know how to look after my master's interests, so of course I took good care to have such a marriage as he wanted come off in the wrong place.

GREEN. What place was that?

BARNEY. Faith! The wrong place for a Scottish marriage is the English side of the Scottish line.

ARTHUR. Do you mean to say that the inn you took us to was on the border, but not in Scotland? *(Goes to* BARNEY, *appalled.)*

BARNEY. Of course, I do, sir.

ARTHUR *(frenzied).* You miserable, dastardly villain, I could kill you! *(He grasps him by the throat.)*

BARNEY *(pleading).* But sir, I only followed your orders to the letter. Didn't you come to me all of a sudden one night at the old tavern at Blackburn, and didn't you say, "Barney, I want to get married to onst in Scotland"?

ARTHUR. I did, you rascal!

BARNEY. Didn't ye tell me to take ye to the borders?

ARTHUR. I did. Well?

BARNEY. Well, sir, so I did. To the borders of matrimony, as I thought ye intended.

ARTHUR *(shaking him).* Idiot! Scoundrel! Wretch! Hazel dishonored *(Steps back.)* —and by me—by me! Oh, this is horrible!

(GREEN *interferes, saying "Travers, Travers." In agony* ARTHUR *turns away.)*

GREEN. There's something better to be done now.

ARTHUR. Yes, you are right. We will go find a curate, and I will marry her at once. *(To* BARNEY.*)* Imbecile! I'm about to take measures partially to amend the outrage you have committed. Tell my wi—yes, before heaven, she is my wife—tell my wife that I have been called away, but will return soon. And understand, not a word of this to anyone.

BARNEY. Oh, master, I did not mean—I mean—no sir, not for the world!

ARTHUR. Come then, let us hurry! Every instant now is torture until Hazel is my wife.

(Exit ARTHUR *and* GREEN.*)*

BARNEY. Faith, thin, I can't make this out for the life o' me. He's lost his head as well as his heart, and to a peasant's child, too. *(Looks off.)* Eh—who's this coming up the walk? It's Squire Rodney. That bodes this house no good. Holy murther! Who's that behind him? If it isn't Lady Travers herself! The powers protect us—she's found us out! What shall we do—what shall we do?

(Enter RODNEY, *followed by Lady Travers, old, very ill, leaning on* RODNEY's *arms.)*

RODNEY. This is the place, my lady.

LADY TRAVERS. Barney, is that you?

BARNEY. Yes, your ladyship, I belave it is. I'm not quite sure.

LADY TRAVERS. I thought you were abroad with my son?

BARNEY. Yes, ma'am, I'm with your son, and sure I bane abroad too—leastways, I don't feel at home.

LADY TRAVERS. Is my son here?

BARNEY. No, my lady.

LADY TRAVERS *(aside).* So much the better. Is the lady of the house in?

BARNEY. Is it Lady Carringford ye mane, my lady?

LADY TRAVERS. It is not Lady Carringford that I mean.

BARNEY. She knows all! She is in, my lady.

LADY TRAVERS. Inform her that a lady would speak with her on important business.

BARNEY. I will, my lady.

LADY TRAVERS. Stay—not a word of who it is.

BARNEY. Oh, not for the world, my lady.

LADY TRAVERS. You may go.

BARNEY. Thankee. Faith! I wish I were anywhere out o' this! *(Exit.)*

LADY TRAVERS. Mr. Rodney, I deem it best I should see this girl alone.

RODNEY. Yes, madam, you are right—I shall wait outside. Be kind to her, Lady Travers, for the wrong is not of her doing.

LADY TRAVERS. You're sure her marriage to my son—

RODNEY. Alas, my lady. It was none at all—none at all.

LADY TRAVERS. Thank heaven for that! You may go and wait for me at the hotel.

RODNEY. I will, my lady. Oh, madam, Heaven will bless you for this day's work. *(He exits.)*

LADY TRAVERS. His blessings are worse than any curse! I am helpless and must have his aid. Why is the girl so long in coming?

(Enter HAZEL.)

HAZEL. You wished to see me, Madam?

LADY TRAVERS. I did, please be seated near to me. *(Aside.)* The old story, the fatal power of a handsome face!

HAZEL *(aside as she gets chair).* What a strange commanding tone! I wonder who she is?

LADY TRAVERS. I am Lady Travers. *(HAZEL starts.)* You need not fear me; I have not come to curse, but to beg.

HAZEL. To beg of me? But why, madam?

LADY TRAVERS. Because in your hands lies the honor of an old and noble family. I see in your eyes the womanhood that has so bewitched my son. And to that womanhood, I beg, beseech, implore a fearful sacrifice from you.

HAZEL. Madam, ask any sacrifice I can make in honor, and I will gladly make it for your son.

LADY TRAVERS. Alas! You know not what you promise. Listen! My father had a ward whose fortune he wrongfully used and lost. Upon his dying bed he confessed this to me, and made me promise to hide his shame by marrying our only son to this ward. I promised, and have lived since but to keep my word and save our honor.

HAZEL. Oh, how terrible.

LADY TRAVERS. My son never knew why I was so determined to make this match, but he, to humor me, promised to marry Lady Maud. Suddenly I heard he was living here with you. With grief and shame I gathered strength enough to drag myself here, to implore you to save us all.

HAZEL. Oh, what can I do? What can I do?

LADY TRAVERS. Within a month Lady Maud will come of age and demand a settlement of her estate. Nothing but her marriage to my son can save him from ruin and shame.

HAZEL. Oh, how horrible!

LADY TRAVERS. Leave him—leave him at once.

HAZEL. And never see him again? No, no, you ask more than I have strength to do—besides, what use is it? I am his wife.

LADY TRAVERS. What if you were not his wife?

HAZEL. Ah, then, perhaps Heaven would give me the courage to fly for his sake.

LADY TRAVERS. It will *(Rises.),* heroic girl, for he is free—you are not his wife!

HAZEL. Not his wife? Oh, how terrible!

LADY TRAVERS. As he has deceived me by loving you, so he has betrayed you by a pretended marriage.

HAZEL. 'Tis false! I'll not believe it! Give me the proof!

LADY TRAVERS. Ah! Have mercy or I shall die! Have courage, child! *(Sways —gasps.)*

HAZEL. Courage for what? No, never! He shall right my wrong. He shall make me his honorable wife or I will—

LADY TRAVERS. Stop, child, stop!

HAZEL. I see it all! It is my father's curse, my father's curse! You have asked me to go for his sake, the sake of the man who has so degraded me. Here is my answer. *(Takes off jewelry, puts it on table.)* I accepted these as token of love, given to an honored wife. I scorn them now. I scorn them all. *(About to take off wedding ring, stops.)* — No, not this. My marriage ring! *(Kisses it.)* This I have bought with a wife's love, a woman's perdition. This I will keep. *(Going.)* The rest I leave forever—I go to cover up his infamy with my shame—and may heaven forgive you all! *(She exits.)*

(LADY TRAVERS collapses and falls back in her chair. ARTHUR enters and sees jewelry on table, LADY TRAVERS in chair, as the curtain falls.)

CURTAIN

MUSIC NOTE. *During* HAZEL's *final speech, music starts. At beginning, it is a slow soft funeral dirge. Then it leads into "Goodbye, the Golden Links of Love Are Broken".* A barbershop quartet in formal evening dress can come on R. and sing:*

> *Goodbye, the golden links are broken,*
> *Goodbye, the parting words are spoken,*
> *Goodbye, you have back every token,*
> *Goodbye, goodbye, I leave you now, sweetheart, goodbye!*

They hum during the rest of her speech, then at end of speech they sing:

> *Goodbye, goodbye, I leave you now, sweetheart, goodbye!*

If preferred, HAZEL *can sing "Goodbye" solo, at the end of her speech, before she says, "And may heaven forgive you all!"*

*Music on page 156.

ACT THREE

SCENE ONE

SCENE: *Evening, kitchen at Blackburn Mill. The door is lit by glow of fire. A clothes-drying rack with towels on it sits before the fire. There is a clock and cupboard, in which are pipe, matches, tobacco, food, dishes; a lighted candle on table.* MERCY *is discovered at table U.C. Lights are half down; clock strikes eight.*

MERCY. Eight o'clock. Time for evenin' prayers—now to put awa' the linen. *(She puts away in drawers outside. Pipe is heard playing.)* What's that? Strange! Met used to play that tune, and it sounds like Met, too. What can it mean? Has she left Hazel? Aye, perhaps she's come with her. Met! Met! Is that you? Met! Met! It is you!
(Enter MET, *U.L., pale, ragged and haggard.)*
Come in, girl, and tell me the news! What's the word? Speak, girl, speak!
MET. I want her—where is she?
MERCY. Who?
MET. Hazel—I want her—I've tramped four hundred miles to find her.
MERCY. My heart, lass! What are ye sayin'?
MET. I must see Hazel—she's here.
MERCY. Hazel here? No, she's not here.
*(*MET *staggers to a chair.)*
Mercy on us, what's coom to thee?
MET. Not here? Where can she be, where can she be?
MERCY. Wi' her hoosband, I suppose.
MET. No, no, she left him a month ago.
MERCY. Left him! Why?
MET. I don't know—I don't know.
MERCY. Where did she go?
MET *(seated).* Why, I thought she'd coom here, so I followed her on foot *(Rises.),* but I'll go back again. I'll walk till I die, but I'll find her.
MERCY. Ah, what do you mean, Met, what do you mean?
MET. Mean? I mean there's something wrong. That man's mother came to the house—she was found dead there and Hazel gone.
MERCY. Great heavens, Met! You frighten me!
MET. Hazel is somewhere wandering now as I have been for a month—ill, cold, starving, perhaps, as I am! But I'll go to her; I must. I will find her.
MERCY. Stop—I'll go wi' thee, lass.
MET *(takes her hands).* Oh, mistress, heaven will bless you for that word.
MERCY. But you must wait until after prayers; Dunstan would miss me if I went off now; he'd ask questions, and oh, Met, he must not know—he's been very ill—this news would kill him.

MET. Then, mistress, you go to the master. I'll run down to Squire Rodney's house. If I can find him he will help me.

MERCY *(picks up lantern and follows her to the door)*. Aye, so he will. Then go, go quickly; I will meet you at his house within an hour.

MET. Never fear, missus, we'll find her now for sure. *(Exit.)*

MERCY. So we will—so we will. *(Hangs up lantern and exits.)*

(PITTACUS enters. ARTHUR follows.)

ARTHUR. Well?

GREEN. Not a soul in sight. All is quiet as the grave.

ARTHUR. Look yonder, she may be inside. Well? *(GREEN opens door U.R., draws back and removes his hat.)*

ARTHUR *(removing his hat)*. And Hazel?

GREEN. Is not among them.

ARTHUR. Oh, shall I never find her? Never see her precious face again?

(DUNSTAN's voice is heard in closing verses of a psalm.)

GREEN. Their prayers are over now; they'll soon be here, and when they come, we'll ask them if they have heard anything of your—of her.

ARTHUR. I have searched for her everywhere without discovering a trace. My last hope has been to find her here. If we fail now, I shall believe the worst.

GREEN. And what is that?

ARTHUR. That she has taken her own life—murdered by me! Oh, the thought will drive me mad!

(GREEN, rising, follows him, pacifying, and pats him on the shoulder.)

GREEN. Merciful powers!

ARTHUR. What is it?

GREEN. We forget—they'll recognize you!

ARTHUR. And if they do?

GREEN. The old miller hates you! If he knows where Hazel is, you are the one man in the world he'll keep her hidden from.

ARTHUR. What are we to do?

GREEN. Leave me till Dolly comes, and when once I set her tongue at work, we'll soon know. Go, wait outside until I have a chance to make her talk.

ARTHUR. You'll find me at the seat near the lock. The moment you get news.

GREEN. I'll fly like lightning to tell you all.

ARTHUR. If I find her not this time I shall despair, I shall despair. *(He exits.)*

GREEN. Poor fellow, he's broken-hearted, and yet it would do no good to tell him till we find Hazel, and I can prove what I suspect about old Rod.

DOLLY *(offstage)*. All right, aunt, I'm going.

GREEN. Dolly's voice! She's coming! She'll see me! The shock might shake her. *(He leaves gloves on table and hides behind clothes-drying rack.)* I'll retreat and spare her feelings for a while.

(Enter DOLLY.*)*

DOLLY. And don't forget to tell Squire Rodney that Uncle Kirke wants to see him here tonight. *(*DOLLY *goes to table, sees glove.)* Dear me! What's this?—a glove! Whose glove? *(Smells.)* Pittacus! *(Turns glove.)* As sure as I'm a woman! So he's been here and gone away without a word!

*(*GREEN *looks out, unseen by* DOLLY.*)*

Oh, that's just like the heartless brute—six weeks since he left me, promising to go and see Hazel and send me news of her; not a word since then. *(Tearfully.)* Oh, these men! these men! Why are they ever made? I can't see the use o' the faithless things.

*(*GREEN *comes up behind her. She continues crossly.)*

Oh, don't I wish I had him here now, how I'd make his ears burn and his head ache!

*(*GREEN *dodges behind clothes rack.)*

How I'd warm his cheeks for him!

(She slaps glove across her hand, then puts it in her apron pocket. Takes clothes from the rack, slams them into basket. While she does so, GREEN *dodges behind remaining clothes in an attempt to hide.)*

The base, deceitful hypocrite! Pretending he couldn't live a day without me! *(Slams towel in basket.)* And then leaving me here *(Slams another towel in basket.)* for weeks and weeks *(Same.)* with a breaking heart!

*(*GREEN *snatches the last towel.)*

Mercy! Who's that?

(Recoiling to chair at right of table, she tips it over and falls. There, as she stares up at GREEN, *he peers over at her.)*

What! So you're there, Mr. Green?

GREEN. No, Dolly, I'm not there, I'm here. And I'm not Green, I'm blue—truly blue, to see you so severe. *(Kneels to her.)*

DOLLY *(moves away, leaving him kneeling).* Don't! Don't touch me, sir!

GREEN. Dolly, Dolly, I say! *(Rises and follows her.)*

DOLLY *(moves about the room paying no attention to him).* Who cares what you say?

GREEN. But, Dolly, I want—

DOLLY. Who cares what you want?

GREEN. But really, my darling—

DOLLY. Don't dare to "darling" me—after—after what's happened!

GREEN. What's happened?

DOLLY. Oh, you know well enough. *(Slaps glove on table.)*

GREEN. Don't jag my glove in that manner! *(Aside.)* Ah, I see, Hazel's been here and told Dolly everything and she thinks I've been an accomplice in this infernal business. Don't, Dolly, don't.

Pittacus pleads with Dolly to be more understanding, as he tries to unwind a snarl in the plot in this third act scene. Pittacus is Robert Montilla; Dolly is Gail Allen.

DOLLY. Don't what, sir?

GREEN. Don't hold me to blame for what's happened—I swear I've spent every spare moment trying to straighten out all this mess and get back to you—and you'll soon find I'm not the man to blame.

DOLLY. Not the man who deserted me all these weeks? *(Aside.)* He is not the man, and he says this to my face. Oh, you brazen rogue!

GREEN. It wasn't me who did it—it was Barney—Barney O'Flynn and that villain, Aaron Rodney! And if Hazel's told you—

DOLLY. Hazel tell me? How could she tell me anything?

GREEN. Then she isn't here?

DOLLY. I haven't seen her blessed face for over a year—and never will see it again, I'm afraid.

GREEN. Hasn't Hazel been here? Has she been—

DOLLY. Here?

GREEN *(stammering)*. Don't you know?—No, she don't!

DOLLY. Know what?

GREEN *(stuttering)*. I—I mean that she must be—I that n-n-nothing!

DOLLY *(fiercely)*. Pittacus—you're deceiving me! Something's happened, don't deny it.

GREEN. I don't—yes—I don't—no—I do.

DOLLY. Where's Hazel?

GREEN. Bless me—that's—that's what I wanted you to tell me.

DOLLY. Then you don't know where she is?

GREEN. No, ding it! I wish I did.

DOLLY. Haven't you see her, then?

GREEN. Oh, yes, that is, no—not since—I say, I saw, I saw that I see, saw—Oh, what am I see-sawing about? I say that I see, that I saw that I see—

DOLLY. Not since when?

GREEN. Well, if you will have it—not since she ran away.

DOLLY. Ran away—from whom?

GREEN. From here—that is—

DOLLY. From her husband, you mean?

GREEN. Y-yes, I suppose I do.

DOLLY. Suppose you do? Don't you know he's her husband?

GREEN. I don't. I only know that life's a nuisance, and it's a swindle I was ever born. *(Sits.)*

DOLLY. Pittacus, Pittacus *(Kneeling to him.)*, what do you mean? What's come to Hazel? Why has she run away—and why do you talk to me so strangely?

GREEN. Dolly, my darling—don't look so miserable—and I'll try to tell you. You see—

DUNSTAN *(offstage, calling)*. Dolly, Dolly! child!

DOLLY. That's Dunstan! He's wanting me—hurry—tell me quick.

GREEN. No—not now—he'll come and hear me and he must never know. I must run, dear—meet me outside near the old tree, as soon as you have found out what he wants. *(Rises, starts to go.)*

DOLLY. All right, I'll come to you the moment I can get away from uncle.

DUNSTAN *(inside)*. Dolly, child, are you comin'?

DOLLY. Yes, uncle, I'm coming.

GREEN *(detains her)*. Why don't the old bear come to you?

DOLLY. Why, poor dear heart, he's blind.

GREEN. Blind!

DOLLY. Yes, just after you went away he got news of some kind that made him awfully ill. For days he was out of his mind raving about Hazel, and when the fever went away, it left him blind.

DUNSTAN *(appears in doorway, old and broken)*. Why, Dolly, child, what keeps ye so long when thee hears me call?

DOLLY *(runs to him)*. I had work to finish here, uncle.

DUNSTAN. Bring me my pipe, child, I have much thinkin' to do tonight, and nothin' helps me think like my pipe. *(He sits.)*

DOLLY. All right, Uncle dear, I'll bring it to ye.

(DOLLY goes to GREEN, sees him out the door, where he points outside to indicate that she will meet him. She motions "yes." He kisses her loudly and goes out.)

DUNSTAN. What be that?

DOLLY. What's that, Uncle?

DUNSTAN. Tha' noise.

DOLLY. What noise, uncle?

DUNSTAN. 'Twere a noise that sounded like a kiss, girl.

DOLLY *(filling his pipe)*. Oh, it must have been—the sputtering of the fire.

DUNSTAN. The only fire I ever heard spooter like that be the fire o' love, lass. Who's been here?

DOLLY. When, uncle?

DUNSTAN. Joost now.

DOLLY *(hands him his pipe)*. Here's your pipe, Uncle. *(Kneels.)* Will I light it for you? *(She strikes a match.)*

DUNSTAN. Aye, lass, do. I wish thou couldst only light my eyes as easy as thou lightest the pipe. *(She lights it for him.)*

DOLLY. Oh, Uncle, don't talk like that. I can't abide it. *(She puts her arm around his neck and places her cheek against his head.)*

DUNSTAN. There, there, child, I'm a weak old fool to bother you with my burdens. Go, find thy Aunt Mercy, she be above stairs. Tell her I must see her and then get thee to bed.

DOLLY. All right, Uncle. *(Aside.)* I'll not go to bed this night until I've got news of Hazel. *(She exits.)*

DUNSTAN. There's no use; even the pipe can't comfort me tonight.

(HAZEL opens window and looks in. She is pale and ragged. She sees DUNSTAN and pauses.)

I must tell my poor wife a' now. It's hard, bitter hard, to leave the mill—a pauper, too—but it moost be done. Better starvation— death—anything—than more debt to Squire Rodney! Oh, that child of mine—my only bairn—why should she have been her feyther's curse? Oh, my old heart is heavy tonight! Would that I were dead!

(*He sobs.* HAZEL *moans and drops her head on the sill.* DUNSTAN *starts up.*)

Who's there? Someone at the window. Who is it? Is there any one there? That's strange. (*He feels his way toward the window.*)

(*Enter* MERCY.)

MERCY. What art doin' there, Dunstan?

DUNSTAN. I could ha' sworn, wife, that I heard someone at the window.

MERCY. Someone at the window?

DUNSTAN. Aye, I heard a noise like a moan, and then, when it died out, it seemed as though the window was closed, quick and sharp like.

MERCY. What if it were Hazel? Child, I know it is, child, I know it is. Yes, it's my child, my darling, longin' to return! Come, Dunstan (MERCY *takes* DUNSTAN *to his chair.*), sit down, and let me speak to thee. Perhaps I can make thee understand the noise at the window.

DUNSTAN. What dost think it were wife? (*Sits.*)

MERCY. Dost' know what day this be, sweetheart?

DUNSTAN. Thursday, I believe.

MERCY. Yes, Thursday, the tenth day of October.

DUNSTAN. Ah! Ah—a—a!

MERCY. This day two and twenty year ago our Hazel were born.

DUNSTAN. Hist, wife, hist! Don't 'mind me o' that day now.

MERCY (*kneels to* DUNSTAN). Why not, oh, father dear, why not? That were a sweet day to us then.

DUNSTAN. Aye, but it is a bitter day to us now.

MERCY (*rises*). Feyther, what if thy child were at thy door now, longin' to come back to the old house?

DUNSTAN. I'd bid her begone.

MERCY (*backs away*). Oh, Dunstan.

DUNSTAN. I'd point at these sightless eyes and say, "This be thy work." I'd point at thee and say—

(*Wind sounds outside.*)

"Look at thy mother, a beggar wi' thy feyther in the street, thy work, too."

MERCY. What dost mean, Dunstan?

DUNSTAN. I mean, Mercy, wife, that the end be coom. I owe everything we gotten in the world to Squire Rodney—an' debt to him I can bear no longer now. I've sent for him to coom this very night and take possession o' the mill—and tomorrow thee and I an' Dolly moost wander out beggars, but beggars no longer to the man our own flesh and blood has wronged.

MERCY. Oh, Dunstan, can ye never forgive?

DUNSTAN. Never!

(*The wind sounds.*)

Strangers she chose; to strangers let her look, for she be dead to us forever.

(HAZEL *moans and drops her head.* DUNSTAN *starts.*)

Hark—that moan again!

MERCY *(going to the window).* Aye and see—the window's open! Oh, Dunstan, what if it be our child, our Hazel!

DUNSTAN. Hoot, woman, it were the wind!

(The wind sounds again.)

There's a storm comin' up. Maister Rodney 'ull not be here tonight. Better lock up the mill. Close the window, wife, and bolt the door, then get thee to bed.

*(*MERCY *goes to window and looks out.* DUNSTAN *feels his way to the door.)*

Mercy, I'll go once more over the old mill I've loved so long and these hands have tended so well. Goodnight, wife, goodnight.

MERCY. Good night, Dunstan, and may the angels be wi' you, this last night i' the old mill.

*(*DUNSTAN *exits.)*

An' my child may be out in the night—homeless and hungry! No, no, I'll go for Maister Rodney. He will save Hazel, an' he's able to break the iron o' her fayther's will. *(Exit, weeping.)*

*(*HAZEL *appears at window. Then slowly opening the door, she steals wearily in and shivers over the fire.)*

HAZEL. Oh, how cold I am. But no fire will ever warm me again. *(Looking about.)* And this is the home, the home that I have lost, the home that I have cursed. My father's chair! How often have I sat upon his lap, my arms around his neck and heard him sing his dear old songs! How often have I knelt here at my mother's feet and prayed as I can never pray again! *(She sinks on her knees by the chair.)* Oh, father, father, Heaven has heard your curse.

(With a sob, she buries her face in chair. DUNSTAN *appears, R. He gropes across the room, places his hand on the back of the chair where she kneels. She draws back; he starts.)*

DUNSTAN. What be that?

(The wind sounds.)

Nothing but the sobbing of the storm. Ah, it does me good to hear it. It sounds like the voice of my own heart. Dear old mill, my eyes will never—no, never more behold thee *(He goes from place to place touching.)* and my hands have felt thy timbers for the last, last time.

*(*HAZEL *follows him across the room, removes a chair from his path, kisses the lapel of his coat.)*

But God's will be done! God's will be done!

(He gropes his way to the door L., lifts his hands in prayer, and exits D.R. HAZEL *goes back and bows her head on the arm of the chair.* RODNEY *enters U.L. He is warmly dressed against the storm.)*

RODNEY. Ah, a fearful night! Is that you, Dolly? So—Hazel, you've come back! Can it be that you have seen the error of your ways?

HAZEL *(rising)*. Don't speak to me! Let me go—away from here, forever!

RODNEY *(stopping her)*. Let you go now? Never!

HAZEL *(turning to him)*. But you do not know!

RODNEY. Yes, Hazel, I know all. I know that when you broke your promise to me, you went to the arms of an unscrupulous villain, who deceived and dishonored you. But see, we are willing to forgive you. Your mother's arms, your father's home—yes, even I am willing to take you back.

HAZEL. Mr. Rodney, you know not what you say. My father but now, a moment ago, declared that he would never own me again in this world. Tomorrow he leaves this dear old mill, driven hence by my broken promise, by my own shame.

RODNEY. Dunstan quit the mill?

HAZEL. Alas, sir, who can prevent it now?

RODNEY. You, girl.

HAZEL. I? Impossible! He would never accept a service from such as I.

RODNEY. Yes, one service, that would pay his debt to me.

HAZEL. What is that?

RODNEY. Keep your promise and become my wife.

HAZEL. Sir, I am an outcast—dishonored—you would marry me?

RODNEY. Indeed, girl—I would—and soon! *(Aside.)* I must convince her or all will be lost! *(To HAZEL.)* I know you thought you loved that scoundrel, but now that you've found him out—reprent your folly and keep your promise to me!

HAZEL. Oh, what shall I do, what shall I do?

RODNEY. Marry me—save your father—promise you'll do this.

HAZEL. I will—on one condition.

RODNEY. And what is that?

HAZEL. Call my father—he is blind—he cannot see me. If he consents to let me pay his debt, you shall have my hand and I will be your wife.

RODNEY. I'll call him instantly. Wait here.

*(*RODNEY *goes toward the door.* DUNSTAN *enters.)*

DUNSTAN. Why, Mr. Rodney, is that you, sir? I did not think you'd coom in this fearful storm.

RODNEY. You sent for me—I was delayed, but here I am. Tell me— what is it, Dunstan?

DUNSTAN. Maister Rodney, for five long years I've been in debt to you *(He sits.)*, a debt I thought my child would pay, but—well—when she broke faith and left us, I strove hard to make the old mill earn enough to pay the money I owed ye. Fever laid hold on me and left me blind. All hope is over for me now—and so I've called ye to ask one more favor of ye—take the mill, but spare poor Mercy and me.

Let us live out our miserable years in peace in this old home—

RODNEY *(crossing to* DUNSTAN*).* But Dunstan, you needn't lose the mill.

DUNSTAN. Yes, I must, for I and mine have wronged ye in every way. I'll do penance for my child as a beggar in the street.

RODNEY. Let Hazel do penance for herself. Let her pay the debt by marrying me.

DUNSTAN. What do ye mean, man?

RODNEY. I mean, Hazel is free!

DUNSTAN. Free o' what? The stains o' shame? *(Rises and crosses to fireplace.)* No, she can never pay any debt o' mine.

RODNEY. Dunstan, it is the only way, hear me!

DUNSTAN. Never—not one word!

*(*HAZEL *kneels before him.)*

If she were here now, before my very face, kneeling at my feet, praying for my consent to marry ye,—I'd tell her nay, never! I'd tell her she had wronged ye bad enough without seeking to make ye hoosband to a dishonored creetur like herself!

(The wind moans. HAZEL *sinks to the floor.)*

RODNEY. So you'll not consent to have her marry me? *(He lifts her and places her in chair.)*

DUNSTAN. Never!

RODNEY. Then I'll marry her without your leave! I'll speak to Mercy and have her consent.

DUNSTAN. That ye'll not, sir, and mind this—Mercy has given her word not to set eyes upon her child without my consent. She'll not lie, not even to please you, Maister Rodney, and so good night, good night, Maister Rodney, good night. *(Exit.)*

RODNEY. Oh, hard-hearted man! May the devil curse your iron-will and break its strength forever! Hazel, don't mind that now. All the world knows that a mother's love—Hazel!

HAZEL. Mr. Rodney, do you want me still?

RODNEY. More than life—or all the world!

HAZEL. Then leave me for now. Leave me and let me be alone for tonight. Tomorrow will settle all for the best.

RODNEY. Must I leave you then?

HAZEL. If you care for my happiness.

RODNEY *(kisses her hand).* Then until tomorrow—tomorrow when we'll be together. Good night my darling; I hear your mother coming; you can rest on her heart tonight and be at peace. Good night, Hazel. *(Exit.)*

HAZEL. All is over. I know the worst now, and I know what I must do. I'll go, and there in the water that has brought so much misery to this home, I'll drown my sorrows and my sins. *(Going.)* Good-bye, old home—farewell, sweet memories, fond hopes—farewell, mother, father, life—life—life!

(She goes out. The wind moans louder. After a pause, DUNSTAN *speaks outside.)*

DUNSTAN. Mercy, Mercy, where be ye? *(Entering.)* Why don't ye answer me? Mercy has gone, where can she be? Oh, why don't ye answer? No one here, the house deserted! What can it mean?

MET *(outside).* Help! Help! She's drowning. *(*MET *enters.)* Drowning! Hazel's drowning! I saw her jump in—it's Hazel, Hazel! *(Rushing across at back.)* Hurry, help, help! *(Exit U.R.)*

DUNSTAN *(in horror).* Hazel, drowning! Dying! Here, before my face? No, no, I'll save her! Ah, heaven! I cannot! I am blind! *(Falling on his knees.)* Oh, God! This is thy punishment! I was blind when I drove her out—and now, when I could save her—I cannot see—I cannot see—I cannot see! *(He falls to the ground and kneels with clasped hands and face upturned in agony.)*

CURTAIN

SCENE TWO

SCENE: *Same as Scene One. It is the following morning; the fire is out; the table is cleared; a jug of water and a mug are on the table.* DOLLY *is discovered asleep in a chair, head in arms. Enter* GREEN *with cigarette.)*

GREEN. Dolly! Dolly! How lovely she looks—yes, a veritable sleeping beauty; but her time has come—the prince is here, and will wake her with a kiss. Will you permit me? Of course she will.

(He kisses her, DOLLY *makes a motion as though brushing away a fly. He kisses her again.)*

She's the kind of a fish that won't rise at a fly. Fire in the shape of a kiss is a failure—we'll try smoke. *(He blows smoke in her face.)*

DOLLY. Pah! *(She awakes with a sneeze.)* Smoke—Where's the fire?

GREEN. Here—here—in my breast—consuming my heart for you.

DOLLY. Oh, Pittacus, I'm so glad you've come! I have so much to tell you! Such strange things have happened!

GREEN. I adore strange things—that's why I adore you *(He embraces her).*

DOLLY. Hush—my aunt—

*(*MERCY *enters.)*

MERCY. At last he seems to be asleep. What, you here, Mr. Green?

GREEN. Well, madam, you may not believe it, but I rather think I am.

MERCY. And Hazel, my child, have you news of her?

GREEN. Well, you see—that is—does she know the truth?

DOLLY. Nothing from me.

MERCY. Well, sir, can't you answer me?

GREEN. Yes, of course—that is—I could if you—I—we—only knew what you meant.

MERCY. Something terrible has happened—I feel it in my heart—but I am so dazed with grief. I can't quite make it out. Last night Met appeared, told me Hazel had left her husband and could not be found. I promised to meet her at Aaron Rodney's house. I went there late last night. Neither Met nor Maister Rodney were there. I hurried home and found my husband dangerously ill. What happened while I was gone, I cannot say, but I think Hazel must have come and—

GREEN & DOLLY *(eagerly)*. Well, well?

MERCY. I fear he heard her—had a fit of rage, drove her out again, and was struck down by the power of his passion.

GREEN. Impossible! If Hazel had been here she would not have gone without a word to you.

MERCY. It's hard to think it, and yet, I cannot tell—I cannot tell.

(RODNEY enters.)

Ah, thank heaven! Maister Rodney, have you seen Hazel?

RODNEY. Certainly—here.

ALL. Here?

MERCY. Then she is coming!

RODNEY. Coming? Has she gone?

DOLLY. We do not know.

GREEN. Great heavens! I see it all—she's with Carringford!

MERCY. Her husband?

GREEN. Yes, he came down here with me last night to look for her. When I returned to our lodgings, he was not there. I didn't mind it, for ever since she left him, he's had a fashion of wandering out at night till very late.

DOLLY. Yes, go on.

GREEN. When I woke this morning, he was still not in his rooms.

DUNSTAN *(offstage)*. Water! Water!

MERCY. Hark! 'Tis Dunstan!

DUNSTAN *(appears in doorway)*. Water—Water—Water!

RODNEY. What does this mean?

MERCY. Ah—he's raving again!

(DUNSTAN enters.)

DUNSTAN. Quick—water, water—I'm burning up! This is the lake that burneth forever—remorse, remorse, remorse! Water—no, no—take it away—'twas water killed her.

RODNEY. What's that he says?

DUNSTAN. Hark—I hear that cry again! Oh, God—save her—save her—she's drowning, drowning!

ALL. Drowning!

DUNSTAN. Yes, she was drowned! I did it—I held her till she died—I couldn't help it. Something forced me on. What was it? What was it? This hard, hard, heart of mine. See, see? There she goes to the mill—

she beckons me! Quite right, lass, quite right. Yes, take me to the mill, take me to the mill! The noise will drown the awful voices here, here. Yes, child, I'm coming—coming—*(He exits D.R.)*

GREEN. And this is the bitter end of all! No, no—there's something still to do, a duty that must be done.

MERCY *(starting up)*. Where are ye going?

GREEN. To search for Hazel—'neath the mill stream.

MET *(rushes in)*. Mistress—oh, mistress!

(MERCY embraces her.)

MERCY. Hark! 'Tis Met! She must have news of her!

MERCY. Where is she, lass? Where is she?

MET. Coming here with her husband! God bless him! God bless him!

MERCY. Heaven be praised!

MET. Last night when she fell in the river—I called for help and jumped in. The river was running strong, and when I caught her in my arms, she was unconscious. I was growin' faint and beginnin' to despair—when I saw him standin' on the bank. I shouted; he heard and plunged in!

MERCY. My child drowning!

GREEN. Go on—go on!

MET. Ah, it's a stout heart and a strong arm he has—Hazel's hoosband! He landed us both near Deacon Woodford's house. There he took us, and brought us back to life.

MERCY. Thank heaven! Thank heaven! *(She weeps with joy.)*

(HAZEL appears L., followed by ARTHUR. DOLLY crosses to HAZEL.)

HAZEL *(holding out her arms)*. Mother! Mother!

MERCY *(embracing her)*. My child—my own precious child! *(To ARTHUR.)* You've earned the right to call my Hazel "wife," and I can't help knowing thee'll be good to her and honor her, sir. And surely now her father must forgive thee both!

(All gather round MET, who is dancing with happiness.)

ARTHUR. I pray he will, for she's never ceased to grieve—tho' I've done all I know to make her happy. Oh, Green, this is a happy day, but I thank heaven my mother never lived to see it.

GREEN. Why so, Arthur?

ARTHUR. I told you of the shame that was overhanging our house?

GREEN. You did.

ARTHUR. Well, I ordered my solicitors to settle my estate, and satisfy every claim of Lady Maud's against my grandfather, if it took every penny I had in the world. He observed my orders, and there remains to me now—

GREEN. Nothing?

ARTHUR. Nothing but my own hand, my own brains, and the endless wealth of my love for her—my beloved wife.

RODNEY. Wife! This farce has gone too far! Madam, I had tried to spare you this—knowing the burden you already bear—a faithless daughter, failing mill, and Dunstan gone blind, but it is time you knew the truth about this man whom you are about to take into the bosom of your home. Not only has he taken your innocent daughter from the protecting arms of her betrothed husband, but he has dishonored her with a false marriage—a base deceit practice with the connivance of his servant, Barney—whose false tongue can be purchased for a shilling!

MERCY. Can this be true?

GREEN *(steps out).* Squire, as a teller of tales myself, your story interests me, but I beg of you, before you go on, I have a tale of my own I'd like to tell. Will you permit me?

DOLLY. Yes, let him tell it.

GREEN. Well, as I once told Miss Dolly, I have great faith in the power of a yarn to undo a snarl, so, since our friend Mr. Rodney here, has put things in such a snarl—*(Crosses, sits on edge of table as storyteller.)* It all begins, as good tales should, with "once upon a time." Our villain, then a young man in his prime, journeyed to London where he proceeded to live in princely style, and nightly visited the gaming tables. But, Capricious Fortune smiled not upon him at the wheel. Instead, her smile came from a woman, not young, not beautiful, but possessed of charms far more appealing to our fair young man. For the spinster, though her locks were gray, had just come into a small fortune. He courted her, married her, and when her funds were nearly gone, bade her fond farewell!

RODNEY. Your tale is entertaining, sir, but hardly at this time.

ARTHUR. No, let him finish.

GREEN. Then, there were others, much the same, all of whom were happy to turn their securities to cash, and all for the honor of earning the prefix "Mrs." But ah, the fleeting days of love! Again he's called away. This time, you truly might not understand: the girl was but a child, untutored, innocent, hardly one to appeal to the jaded tastes of such a man as our hero had become. But wait! She had one virtue in common with all the previous loves—for her inheritance, which would not be hers until she came of age, could be reckoned in figures astronomical! While the other fortunes had been in stocks and bonds, this one was limitless—and this time in diamonds!

RODNEY. Rubbish! I'll hear no more of this.

(He crosses as though to leave. GREEN *and* ARTHUR *restrain him.)*

ARTHUR. You will listen.

GREEN. Yes, you will. You'll hear me out! I've spent months tracking down all the loose threads of the warp, and all the golden strings of Cupid's bow. Squire Rodney, there's a man from Scotland Yard waiting outside for you now!

RODNEY *(pulls gun, steps back).* Stand back! You'll never get me now. I've waited far too long that you should spoil my plans!

(INSPECTOR *enters*. GREEN *and* ARTHUR *struggle to take gun from* RODNEY. *They all push him out the door, still struggling for gun. As they exit, a shot is heard.*)

DOLLY (*rushing to door*). What is it? Are you hurt?

(*Re-enter* GREEN *and* ARTHUR.)

GREEN. 'Tis only justice, Dolly, he is dead!

ARTHUR. Yes, and by his own hand!

(*Enter* DUNSTAN *D.R.*)

DUNSTAN. What's that, Mercy? Mercy, wife, where are you?

HAZEL (*anxiously to* MERCY). He'll not drive me out again?

MERCY. No, child, no. Dunstan, thy child is home.

DUNSTAN. She's alive, saved?

(MERCY *goes to* DUNSTAN. ARTHUR *stands behind him.*)

MERCY. Aye, Dunstan, by her hoosband. The man who took her from thee has brought her back to thy arms.

DUNSTAN. Where is she? Where is she?

MERCY (*arm around* HAZEL *as they cross to* DUNSTAN). Stretch forth thy hands and feel her face.

(HAZEL *kneels*, MERCY *guides* DUNSTAN's *hands.*)

DUNSTAN. Oh, my child.

HAZEL. Yes, thy child, thine only child!

DUNSTAN (*raising her to her feet*). Hazel, Hazel, coom to my arms! Know thy feyther's heart!

TABLEAU, HAZEL, DUNSTAN *and* MERCY *in embrace C.* DOLLY *and* PITTACUS *U.R.* MET *joins* ARTHUR *U.L.* GREEN *steps C., bows.*

GREEN. Will you permit me?—Thank you. 'Twas our way from earliest time, of winding up a play. A kindly custom—actors know its worth. (*Stepping back and indicating scene.*) Peace after pain, and after sadness, mirth.

CURTAIN

Music

UNDERNEATH THE ARCHES

Un - der - neath the arch - es, _____ I dream my dreams a - way, ____

Un - der - neath the arch - es _____ on cob - ble-stones I lay. ____

Ev - ery night you'll find me, _____ tir - ed out and worn, __

Hap - py when the day - light comes creep - ing, her-ald - ing the

dawn, Sleep - ing when it's rain - ing _____ and sleep - ing when it's fine __

I hear the trains rat - tling by a - bove _____ Pave-ment is my

pil - low, no mat - ter where I stray, _____ Un - der-neath the

arch - es, I dream my dream a - way. _____

LILY OF LAGUNA

She's my la - dy love, she is my girl, my ba - by love, She's the girl for sit - ting down to dream, She's the on - ly girl La - gu - na knows. I know she likes me, I know she likes me, be - cause she said so. She is my Li - ly of La - gu - na, She is my Li - ly and my own.

GOODBYE

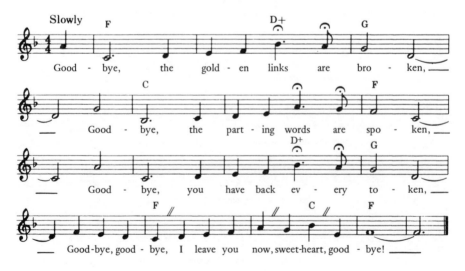

Good - bye, the gold - en links are bro - ken, — Good - bye, the part - ing words are spo - ken, — Good - bye, you have back ev - ery to - ken, — Good-bye, good - bye, I leave you now, sweet-heart, good - bye! —

IF I HAD A WISH

GENTLEMAN'S GENTLEMAN

I'd rath-er be a gen-tle-man's gen-tle-man than a gen-tle-man

on my own, I would-n't want a ti - tle or a throne ____

An - y time I'm feel - ing fri-vo-lous and a-mor-ous, too,

I know lots of court - ly la-dies who like my par-lez - vous.

I could - n't count the no - ac-count counts whose count-ess - es count on

me in-stead, I'm ver-y care-ful not to lose my head ____ And though they

don't in - vite me o - ver to dine, I've got the key to the cel-lar where they

store the wine, I'm a gen-tle-man's gen-tle-man all the time. ____

I would - n't care to be a mar - quis 'cause my life's a

lark as it is, What do I care a - bout the so - cial whirl? ____

Fm | **Bb7** | **Eb** | **Cm**

If the duke can't do the du-ties that the duch-ess re - quires,

F | **Bb**

I'm the guy the duch - ess calls_ to come o - ver and light the fires,

Eb | **Ab** | **Eb** | **Fm** | **Eb**

I nev - er mind when meas-ur - ing suits or pol-ish - ing boots or

F | **Bb** | **Eb** | **Ab** | **G** | **Cm**

mend - ing hose, Where do you think I got this suit of clothes?_

Marcato, slower **Ab** | **A°**

_ And if an Eng-lish lord and la - dy pay a vis - it to Par - ee,

Eb | **C**

I can take the la - dy while the lord is tak - ing tea— I'd rath - er

A tempo
F | **Bb** | **Eb**

be a gen - tle-man's gen - tle - man an - y time. _____

CIGARETTE'S DANCE

Dance

Slow **Bm** | | (⌢) **A**

(⌢) **G** | **F#** | **Bm**

Index